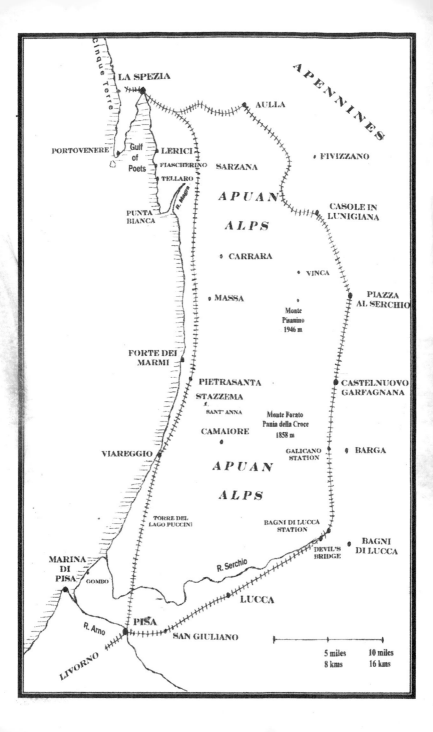

# TUSCAN CAPERS

## A RAIL TRAIL ROUND NORTHERN TUSCANY

*BY THE SAME AUTHOR:*
*THE CAPE TO CAIRO RAILWAY*
*AND RIVER ROUTES*
*and the Grand Hotels*
*en route through Africa.*
*ISBN 978-0-9544847-0-5*

TUSCAN CAPERS
First published in Great Britain in 2011
by Genta Publications,
London SW5
email : gentauk2002@yahoo.co.uk

Illustrated edition
ISBN:  978-0-9544847-1-2

Typeset in Times New Roman.

Printed in Great Britain
by the MPG Books Group,
Bodmin and King's Lynn

# Contents

*List of Illustrations between centre pages:*
Viareggio Liberty Style. Lungarno of Pisa.
Bagni di Lucca Station. Devils Bridge. Uomo Morto.
Fornacetta and Sommocolonia. Spirit of Barga.
Casciani's. Symbol of Survival. Lunigiana.
Relics of Rail Travel. Tellaro Church.
*Front Cover* - Barga

All Photographs by the author except Barga group by P. Laumeier
Design collaboration: D.H Cambridge.

*A Tutti i miei Amici a Barga*

*To All my Friends in Barga*

# PREFACE

A balance of history, combined with modern travel, gives a new slant to such a magnificent area as northern Tuscany. Yet this round trip by rail has to be taken with a pinch or two of salt. It is quite feasible to travel the whole distance in a day, simply by changing trains a couple of times. However a more ambitious few days would be better spent in exploring the hinterland. Unfortunately Italian buses rarely connect with train arrivals; and stations are not always near the towns they represent. So this is not a guide book. It combines local perambulation inspired by the jaunts of the characters that have passed through the centuries. In this land where the grass was always greener on the other side for the British, our literary and artistic history flourished, inspired by the Romantic Poets. In an age before Mass Media, the power of poetry was significant. Tens of thousands of Byron's works were eagerly awaited. Yet there are none more roundly creative than the Italians, in a land blessed with an abundance of God given beauty. So our journey is enlivened with a smattering of poetic verse both local and imported.

In this course through history, it is not possible to avoid the tragic events that engulfed 1943-44. The combined effects of invasion, insurrection, civil conflict and war took their terrible toll. Whilst I have largely confined myself to statements of fact, it would have been unfair not to put into perspective the trauma of those whose lives were so drastically affected. Terrible events tore the place apart as the Resistance fought alongside the Allies to restore democracy and liberty to Italy. Those opposed to the regime of Mussolini engendered little response in recent years. Yet one of the most influential, and perhaps least understood, early godfathers of fascism, was a great Tuscan writer and prolific poet. Gabriele D'Annunzio died long before Italy joined the Axis. He eventually turned his back on them, having made the sublime proposition that music and poetry should be an intrinsic part of the Italian constitution.

To understand history is to understand all. An impossible task.

I am indebted to the many people of that almost untouched and little known part of Tuscany - the Garfagnana region in the foothills of the Apennines - who made this little journey such a enlightened one.

G.P.T.   2011

# *Pre-amble*
## ROME

❧

Tuscany came to me via Rome.

In the 1960's it was the dream city of decadence. After war-weary years, the Roman Spring had arrived. Behind the peeling stucco of neglect, shadows sprang from every street corner like a magic lantern show. It was a magnificent theatre of aspiring young actors. A flood-gate of golden stage lighting working its charm. It was the era of Fellini's celluloid icons. Bronzed aphrodites bathing in fountains. Aristocratic gigolos with slinky dalmatians. Rich ladies in venetian gold, cardinal red and princely purple. Glitteratti pursued by Paparazzi. It was the bitter-sweet era of Roman Holiday and Three Coins in a Fountain.

For some it was a roller coaster ride of *Dolce Vita*. For us it was *Dolce fa Niente* – the sweetness of doing nothing. Like Fellini himself, it was all a big lie.

We were an impoverished band of budding art students, with romantic notions. Few of us had real talent. Most of us we were artist misfits. 'Refugees' of one sort or another. All we shared was 'Italophilia' - a Greek word meaning love of Italy. Our common language was pidgin Italian. Some of us were of the experimental *avant garde* variety. Others, like me, were young traditionalists, with a burning ambition to paint in the style of the Old Masters.

In the stifling heat of that airless Roman summer of our youth, our ambition was to live from day to day, and enjoy freedom to the utmost. The sun was the pull; the prime mover for all of us. All our energy was absorbed by it. It dragged us like moisture from the earth.

Our Art School was named the *Scuola Libera del Nudo* – the free school of the Nude. In a rambling old building, it was part of Rome University.

Although we were free to express ourselves in any way we desired, little else was liberated. Not even the models. There were no other Italians in our section of the Academy. It was strictly for "Stranieri" - loosely translated as 'Diggers in the Jungle'.

There was Jose from Cuba - a cunning, bearded Spaniard, who was as unwieldy as the cigars he smoked. He had escaped Castro's regime with enough money to see him through. Or so he guessed. He was a chain-smoker, yet only occasionally did he drag on the best Havana. Normally he puffed away at those long, spirally, indescribable ones - like himself, fat in the middle and thin at both ends.

There was Miro, a Yugoslavian refugee, who became my good friend. Totally self reliant and utterly ambitious, he had escaped Tito's Yugoslavia across the frontiers to freedom. On a roundabout route he had by-passed border guards, jumped minefields, and scaled razor wire into Trieste. For at that time Italy was one of the few kinks in the Iron Curtain. As a stateless person, he had been holed up in a camp for displaced people, which he called a 'Campo di Concentramento'. Somehow we doubted it. He signed his paintings simply MIRO, and sold 'Big'. Shades of Joan Miro, the Spanish maestro.

Tiger was a naturally nice African, very ebony indeed. Strikingly handsome, with tall classic features and Ethiopian bone structure, he hailed from one of those Italian colonies in the Horniest part of Africa - probably Eritrea or Somaliland. His ambition was to be an airline Pilot. When it came to art, he was adept with Colour - but lacking in Perspective. His drawings of the extremities of the body, such as heads, hands and feet, were out of all proportion to reality. This visual interpretation was politely termed by the Art Professor: "Una Deficenza di Spazio" - a Spatial Deficiency. Somehow I couldn't imagine Tiger landing an aeroplane on a strange runway on a dark winter night.

More famously, for us raunchy romantics, was Inge. She appeared as ultimate 'Posh Totty', with the perfect pouting lips, and legs up to her eyeballs, neatly trimmed in a blue-denim pussy pelmet. The dirty denim look was all the rage. So we all took a shine to this snazzy little Austrian rich bitch, with her up-front Aryan manners and wild red hair.

There was the usual sprinkling of Italophile English ladies. Of slender and delicate proportions. To us, the *jeunesse doré* of the art world, they were a touch jaded. In fact, they were the life-blood, as well as the body and soul of the art experience of Rome. Amazingly practical and talented, English women of the "Room with a View" and "Tea with Mussolini" type had been fussing around Rome for centuries, since long before the days of the Grand Tour when Percy Shelley named Italy 'The Paradise of Exiles'. They fed

3

the stray cats in the old ruins, caused havoc crossing streets, and annoyed the local residents with their eccentric complaints. Yet they were a loveable, endearing part of the landscape, and treated with amused tolerance by the ever-forgiving Italians. Skinny as a rake, they appeared to be more starved of food than the cats they fed. In fact they lived on a voluntary frugal diet of Oxford Marmalade, Marmite, Ceylon Tea and Gentleman's Relish, and all the other preposterous ingredients that homesick English ladies thrive on.

One of them struck me. She was the split image of expatriate Englishness that Fellini had characterised in 'La Dolce Vita'. The languid lady who led the procession through the haunted castle, reciting Dante in husky tones, whilst pursued by the well-bred Schizo, named Steiner. When she finally confronted him, she exclaimed in those deep, throaty tones that only ladies of a certain ilk aspire to: "*Tu sei veramente Primitivo.* You are truly primitive". The poor man shot himself.

There was Miss Mary. She was a governess and a companion to a rich Italian family, who gave the children a 'proper' English upbringing. No one knew her surname, and she was forever known only as 'Miss Mary'. She was Agatha Christie's 'Miss Marple' in disguise. She painted with precision, in delicate strokes from long thin brushes. One always had the feeling she was trying to 'loosen up'. She inspired me to follow in the footsteps of her heroine Mary Shelley. Her ideas came back to haunt me, and drove me to Tuscany.

Visually at least, the most memorable in the Art School was Laura. She was a true Italian bronzed beauty. To my inexperienced eyes, she was the renaissance role model of the perfect female figure. For the six months that I was at the *Scuola Libero del Nudo*, she held court on the model's dais. Aged around thirty, with meercat airs, aquiline nose and proud breasts, she was definitely beginning to show a touch of Rubenesque proportions. I was reminded constantly of Sophia Loren's famous admission: "Everything you see I owe to spaghetti". Whether there was a shortage of female models, or impoverished art students willing to pose, I cannot imagine. For the entire course, we painted nothing but the voluptuous Laura in all her alluring poses. She was a professional, and she knew it. Not to be tampered with under any circumstances. In pencil, chalk, charcoal, watercolour and oil, we laboured away, and immortalised her in every style imaginable. But most exciting of all, for me at least, I captured her, with all her curves and sensual whims, in rich, warm Oil paints. This was my ultimate ambition - to pant ribald nudes like Caravaggio or Botticelli.

Our aged white-haired Professor of Fine Arts was a strict disciplinarian. He ran his class in the Renaissance tradition of a Master overseeing a small group of pupils. Appropriately, his name was Professor Bianchi. He wisely insisted that we only chose four oil colours for our limited palate. These were selected with great deliberation, and stuck to. It was part of the rigid discipline of painting, born of ancient mediaeval restraint. We were allowed one bonus colour - White. Having selected three flesh tints with gay abandon - Yellow ochre, Cadmium red and Raw sienna, I unwisely chose the romantic sounding 'Verde Paolo Veronese' as my fourth colour. Somewhere in the depths of art history, I had learnt that 'a trick of the old masters trade' was to use this particular Emerald Green as an under-glaze, before painting flesh tones on top. A richness and luminescence thus emanated through the shadows. Or so I hoped. I never quite mastered the technique. As a result, all my life-studies ended up with gangrenous looking flesh tones. "Miracoloso!", cried my friend Miro, "Just like that other artist-misfit Van Gogh - always short of the right pigments".

Our model Laura had two maddening habits. The first was changing the colour of her hair at very short notice. At the last stages of one of our oil masterpieces, she would miraculously appear with celestial purple locks - streaked with violent orange or green - colours which few of us could handle.

Laura's other phobias were Peeping Toms. One sunny day, some Italian builders climbed up for roof repairs. Through the high windows, their mesmerised faces suddenly appeared, or rather leered, down at Laura, reclining on the model's dais. She let out a shriek, ran from the platform, down the corridor - stark naked - pursued by the ranting Professor Bianchi..

Our own wild student habits were usually limited to the inevitable problem of how to earn enough money to pay for board and lodging.

Miro and I shared an 'artist's garret' at the top of a seedy old building in Trasteveree. *Tra-Il-Tevere* – "Across the Tiber" - was once the poor mans quarter of Rome; a limbo-land of crafty dealers, small workshops and backstreet doorways where one could obtain almost anything for almost nothing. In spite of its seedy gloss, Trastevere was slowly becoming the fashionable refuge of the Roman Upper Crust.

The garret was up 4 flights of stairs, followed by a climb up a ladder into the attic below the eaves of the roof. You could barely stand in this stifling hell-hole. There were beds at each end. Or rather mattresses lay on the tiled floor. There was no window - only a small opening in the end wall. Through this orifice one could see the roofs of Rome, and the nearby dome of St. Peters - transformed, by the confined optical effect, into a near miraculous sight of majestic proportions.

At night all hell broke loose. Through this tiny opening, mosquitoes swarmed in, mixed with insects and bugs of all descriptions. Even bats appeared, quickly retreating when they realised humans inhabited their eerie. Outside, the night sounds carried on. There was all the bustle and wickedness of nearby streets - the music, the singers. There were cats fighting, dogs barking, babies crying and women shouting at the men who had just dragged themselves from a nearby Taverna. In the early hours, the mist settled, with penetrating dampness. We spluttered to survive, coughing and shivering in turn, to await the dawn of another awesome, blistering day.

Our thirst was one problem. Our dire famine was relieved by Charity. We usually met for lunch at one of the Soup Kitchens run by Nuns. Our favourite haunt was round the corner from the famous Piazza Navona, half way between our Trastevere garret and the Art School. The district was like London's Soho, with smart restaurants springing up everywhere. We mere art students used to sit on the Fountain of the Rivers in the middle of the Piazza, and watch the expensive world pass us by. Envious eyes were cast across the barriers of the restaurants, behind which rich Americans gobbled Saltimbocca Romana's and Osso Buccos, whilst quaffing bottlers of Barolo. In contrast, our Convent Soup Kitchen attracted every conceivable kind of drop-out. We were a well worn bunch of hangers-on. No one was turned away. On arrival, I was unwisely taken by my friend Miro to meet the Mother Superior. She asked me which country I was fleeing from. To have fibbed to a Nun, especially in the Eternal City, would have been the height of decadence, tempting Hell and Damnation. So I took a big yawn and replied laconically "Inghilterra". She was gob-smacked. It was the first, and probably the last time she had heard of anyone escaping from England. I was promptly given one month's trial "period of grace" to prove my good refugee status. In fact there was little to be exploited. From Monday to Friday we were treated to the same simple feasts of spaghetti. This was followed, once a week, by a variable dish of stew, sometimes with a few Nun's leftover chicken bones floating around; but nearly always of beans, vegetables and tomatoes. Meat and fish were otherwise unheard of. The ubiquitous tomatoes were staple fare; those lush ripe juicy ones, which only a sun blessed country like Italy can produce. The soup kitchen naturally did not run to wine. Only water was served, even though wine was far cheaper and easier to obtain. At that time the tap-water in Rome was largely undrinkable. Ancient earthenware sewers still ran alongside equally ancient underground aqueducts. It was the perfect prescription for dysentery, typhoid and cholera. So the worldly nuns brought the water into town by the jar-load, from one of their distant convents in the Alban Hills. It was the most delicious sweet water anyone one could find on earth. And all for free

Before our usually rapid departure, we lined up at a table to be handed two small packets. The first one appeared as reject lifeboat or dog biscuits. These tooth-shattering, tasteless emergency rations were as hard as nuts, only designed to stave off total starvation. The other packet, however, contained two tiny bars of chocolate. Stamped on the back label was the endearing slogan: "Dono del Popolo Americano". Whether this Gift of the American People was part of their generous way of thanking the Allies for liberating them, or simply a devious ploy to keep back some of Europe's roughest refugees, remains a mystery. It was the best PR for the Americans and a Godsend for us Poverini. Those little luxuries saw us through many evenings when we had no other sustenance. It was even possible to barter one for a couple of fags.

On the rare occasions that we sold a painting, we would celebrate in a local *Taverna*. Lashings of wine, bread, cheese and salami were the order of the night. We all joined together at a massive table in the smoke laden atmosphere. It was an international event; Miro and myself, Jose from Cuba, Inge from Austria and sometimes Miss Mary. We inevitably got plastered - *Stuccatto* – as we puffed away at those rough Italian cigarettes called *Esportazione*. One wondered to which country they could possibly be exported.

The day came in July when the Art School finished. Thoughts turned to the prospect of a disagreeable baking summer in Rome. Everyone who was anyone escaped to the seaside. All the offices closed. It was the sort of relentless heat that sucks the energy out of everything. Even the craggy stones walls evaporated before your eyes in that stupor.

Surprisingly, there was no official Art School Exhibition. But the Fiera d'arte di Via Margutta was the sensational highlight of the bohemian art world. It was where the *Jeunesse Dore* met the *Beau Monde* in a kind of Montmartre of Rome. This Art Fair attracted real talent - for a fee. Exhibitors paid handsomely for stand space. Art students paid nothing. We 'strung along' and were actually encouraged to squeeze between the piles of famous artists who lived in this fashionable area, right by the Spanish Steps. More unofficially, we asked the shop keepers to prop our modest works against the doorways of their fancy antique shops. In return we gave them one of our rather insipid views of the Forum or the Coliseum - or some other hackneyed tourist view of the Eternal City.

Amazingly, I ended up selling literally dozens of views of Rome for modest amounts. This was not due to any real talent. Having tired of early attempts to emanate the old masters, I perfected a simple technique of producing pseudo renaissance sketches. They were brown ink drawings washed over with pale watercolour, on moth-eaten brown wrapping paper – the cheaper and older the better. There were lots of pillars, arches and broken marble columns, surrounded by weeds in the foreground, and hills in the background. These creations stood out not for their great draughtsmanship, but for the fact that they were totally different from the usual florid chocolate box views. They had an antique feel, with a jaded, earthy look of architectural coolness combined with old master technique. Some poor punters were fooled. Cool. That is the art market.

My friend Miro was in a different class. He was naturally adept in the art of painting nudes, particularly in the modernistic manner. Whether it was because of his name, or because of his hidden talent, he attracted one or two rich patrons – and so he eventually "arrived". Via Margutta welcomed him with open arms. He was a presentable individual with flair; and, with a name like Miro, who could lose?

Many of the others failed the test, but Inge's efforts were wild and luscious. They were spontaneous figure drawings with an esoteric edge. Flamboyant colours and pithy symbols turned on the heat.

The gay, vivacious, happy-go-lucky crowd of the Via Margutta were of all nationalities and creeds. Freedom of expression also meant freedom of opinion - even though few artists took anything seriously, least of all their art. Most memorable was a well known artist called Marciano Secondo He appeared as an outrageous transvestite, dressed to kill in Roman toga and Imperial hat; a cross between a Vestal Virgin and Nero, complete with painted toenails and lipstick. I never discovered who Marciano the First was.

Flowing togas were all the rage. Americans in droves wore them during the stifling summer months which locked most people indoors from noon till four. For Rome in August was a veritable crucible; an inferno which Dante would not have appreciated, until the afternoon breezes restored the battled senses.

Naturally, we poor art students could not afford to siesta. Our garret in the roof resembled not an attic, but an almost airless Black Hole of Calcutta. We lay on the grass wherever we could and watched the Lorries spray the streets with water jets, sending up volcanic clouds of steam, whilst the army of cleaners swept alongside with long brooms. Rome was dead for the only time in early afternoon

As the buildings and doorways shimmered in the heat, they made me view marble in a new light. Where did it all that cool stone come from, I wondered. How was it hewn from the earth, and where did they find such enduring quality and varied hues. My mind turned once more to Tuscany.

Our favourite hang out was around the Spanish Steps. At one time this worldly location was known as the 'Ghetto of the English'. The Spanish Ambassador of the early 1800's levied local taxes to pay for the paving slabs in the square. It was a hang out for artist's models, as well as all manner of lovely ladies hoping to be picked up and whisked off. As I dozed on the Spanish steps under the noses of the nodding flower sellers I often wondered what it was like back in the 1820's. On one side stood the studio of the almost unknown amateur artist Amelia Curran, whose portrait of Percy Shelley is the only surviving image of him.

On the other side, at the bottom of the steps was the John Keats Museum. As I wandered around the death-place of that doomed young poet who escaped south to avoid the harsh English winter, in the hope of curing his Tuberculosis, I recalled those Odes: To a

Nightingale, To Melancholy, To a Grecian Urn, To a Psyche and To Autumn. They all appeared in 1820. For it was in that last active year of his short life, before he left England, that the energetic young Keats poured out more verse than anyone else in his country's history. The Cockney son of a stable manager from London's East End was far from a simpleton. He saw the sublime in almost everything, and nothing could have been more remotely nostalgic for him than sipping wine and listening to the splashing of Bernini's fountain outside, as he composed his own epitaph "Here lies one whose name is writ in water".

I was determined to discover what motivated those reckless rebels, before they were driven to an early grave. Byron, Shelley and Keats only lived for 20 or 30 years. All three were born, and all three died, within 4 years of each other. Like the ancient heroes, they were destined to die young, to satisfy the decrees of the gods.

**George Gordon, Lord Byron 1788 – 1824.**
**Percy Bysshe Shelley 1792 – 1822.**
**John Keats 1795 – 1821**

Between them they embraced the whole world of romantic verse. What was is that drove these brooding spirits to escape to the sun laden south; not just for health reasons, but to recharge their lyrical and physical batteries at the fountain source of all knowledge. Emotion played a large part in it. For misery and suffering is food for romantic heroes. There must have been something seriously wrong with Italian water - or the wine of the 1820's, to have caused such havoc, and the early demise of such talent.

Other poets came to Italy for escapist reasons. Coleridge stayed for 14 years to avoid his wife - a woman too much like his mother. They were English, but the spirit of Italy ran through their veins

I too was a blithe spirit with wanderlust in my eyes, and time on my hands. Like them, in my early twenties I was already a hardened vagabond, in love with romance and adventure. Impulse and Passion dictated my moves.

Around the Spanish Steps I met my match. With Inge. Her friend Angela was an English artist living in Trastevere.

As near neighbours, very soon we got to know each other. One evening, none too rich in imagination, I pressed the point: "Want to see my paintings?" Surprise! She agreed.

We limbered nimbly up the 4 flights of stairs and then climbed the ladder through the loft door into my garrett. Angela didn't waste much time looking at my paintings. She went straight to the point. Our looks crossed, as she turned invitingly. I sensed something was up. Being young and goal orientated, we vied with each other.

'I frutti proibiti sono I piu dolci'. Forbidden fruit is the sweetest.

Much later we hit it off nicely. Then all of a sudden she went back to England. And Inge went back to Austria.

# Chapter 1

## PISA

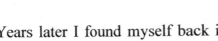

Years later I found myself back in London. I had just returned from travels in Africa. In one of those chance encounters which happen when never expected, I bumped into my Tuscan match. I hadn't seen Inge since my days at the Art School in Rome. Inevitably, it was raining. We darted into the Travellers Bar in one of the grand hotels in Knightsbridge to retrace our bearings. She was well settled but still suffered from wanderlust. "So do I" I added. Most important she was still in touch with Angela. "We are all suffering from Wanderlust. What about making a Grand Tour of Italy? A threesome - just like the poets."

I adjourned to the nearby Gents to collect my thoughts. It was a haven of tranquillity and aged luxury. Edwardian taps spat scalding water into shining marble wash basins like mesmerising marble fountains. There was the usual array of 'smellies' – gold topped bottles of hand wash, and colognes – you name it - a veritable array lined up on the marble slab – yours for the taking. In attendance was Luigi, from somewhere in Italy. The true gentleman's gentleman. 'I have a master and I am his man' was the caption beneath the faded Punch cartoon on the wall beside the doorway. Very appropriately, he handed me a towel, as I withdrew my dripping hands from the swirling waters.

"Just back from abroad, Sir?" he enquired. "Yes – Africa" I murmured.

"Italy had no colonies in Africa," he replied, "to speak of - only Abyssinia and Libya for a while under Mussolini." His knowledge inspired me.

He had noticed my tanned face. He picked up a large, menacing bone-handled clothes brush; then proceeded to dust the last vestige of imaginary fluff off my jacket, with a dash of military precision. With a quick flick, and a slow pause, he leant forward, cupped his hand, and murmured in my ear:

"Natives are getting a bit restless, I believe." He could see I was uncomfortable.

"I'd love to go to Italy" I said, "To escape some of this foul winter weather."

"It's where the English have gone for centuries," he volunteered. "Ever since the days of those great poets. And the Grand Tour?"

"Absolutely!" was my only response.

My connection with Tuscany was cemented.


"Byron and Shelley and Keats - a trio of literary treats," Angela recited that old schoolgirl rhyme.

"The forehead of Byron was covered in curls, and Keats never was the descendant of Earls." She tailed off:

"I've forgotten the rest."

"As far as I can remember it all happened in northern Tuscany - Pisa and Lucca and the coast. But I'm sketchy."

"When Tuscany was under Austrian rule" added

16

Inge. "Let's follow them."

Was it not true that two of the great poets of the age Percy Shelley and Gordon Byron had left England under a cloud? Soon after the Battle of Waterloo in 1815 they went on a Grand Tour of Europe with their girlfriends. Keats had hoped to join them. Shelley had met him through his literary agent, the editor Leigh Hunt, a man with a revolutionary reputation who had been imprisoned for libelling the Prince Regent.

Percy Shelley, the heir to a Baronetcy, came from one of the wealthiest landowning families in England. Known at Eton as "Mad Shelley", he had been sent down from Oxford for writing scurrilous, atheistic articles. He quarrelled with his father, and hastily married his first wife, the 16 year old daughter of a rich London Coffee House & Tavern owner. An exponent of Free Love, in 1814 he conveniently hitched up with the intellectually inquisitive Mary Godwin, who was the daughter of an equally trendy liberal, William Godwin. He was another atheist with zealous views which bordered on anarchy.

Percy and Mary eloped to the continent, where they were joined by Mary's half-sister Claire Clairmont. This was the start of their *Menage a Trois*.

During this first short Grand Tour, they travelled down the Rhine to Switzerland. There they joined up with Gordon Byron, who had rented the Villa Diodati – an extravagant villa with spectacular views over Lake Geneva. This was the start of the *Menagerie*.

The house soon achieved fame for the scandalous goings on between the four of them -

Gordon, Percy, Mary and Claire. The local gossip was so wild that the sharp-eyed proprietor of the nearby Hotel D'Angleterre charged his inquisitive guests large fees to look through a powerful telescope trained directly onto the terraces and open windows of the Villa Diodati.

A year later, Claire gave birth to Gordon's child.

Percy's first wife drowned herself in London's Serpentine. He lost custody of their children, so he was free to hitch up with Mary.

They ran away to Edinburgh and were married in a Kirk by a Minister, who knew that they were under-age. He was later transported to Australia for similar 'ecclesiastical discrepancies'.

Percy claimed that 'Poets were the unacknowledged legislators of the world'. His word was powerful. He had already rallied the early pioneers of the Trade Union movement with his pen, all the way from Italy:


**Men of England, Heirs of Glory; Heroes of Unwritten Story**
**Rise like lions after slumber, in unvanquishable number...**

*The Mask of Anarchy 1819.*

He urged them on to demonstrate, in response to the news of the Peterloo Riots in Manchester, - that sorry saga when simple workers, dressed in their

Sunday best, peacefully protesting for parliamentary reform, had been cruelly beaten down by the Cavalry.

Whilst the more liberal Percy Shelley was on the side of the underdog, Gordon Byron considered servants fair game for an English Aristocrat. At the age of twenty he had already fathered his first child by a lusty housemaid at his English country estate. At the same time he was indulging in a nefarious affair with his page-boy, the under-age son of a local tenant farmer.

He gave more than a modest sum for his child Lucy, the housemaid's daughter, who was raised by relatives. As a young girl she was later employed by Byron, who insisted she dress up and act as a page-boy.

The straw which finally broke the camel's back was when he had been found shagging his half sister Augusta, whilst her husband Colonel Leigh was away gambling and living it up at Newmarket races. (Augusta and Gordon had the same father). The whole of England was agog with gossip.

He was eventually driven from out of the country by a catty coterie of prying eyes and wagging tongues. Invited by a prominent Mayfair hostess, he arrived at a farewell party with Augusta, only to be left propping the mantelpiece in the drawing room with his hostess and his mistress, after a mass walk-out of the assembled guests. Yet he was still the darling of the upper classes. With the haughty classic looks of a Greek God, and in spite of his club foot, he continued his adulterous love affairs with the beauties of London Society. As a token of her love, Lady Caroline Lamb sent this 'Mad, Bad and Dangerous to know' paramour a few curls of her pubic hair. She begged Gordon to repay her in the same way, though warning him to be careful not to cut himself.

To escape the tittle-tattle, Gordon set off for Italy on his next, even more extravagant, Grand Tour. As usual, his reputation had leapt in bounds before him. He had commissioned an opulent travelling coach which was modelled on Napoleons robust 'Campaign Chariot'. All his carriages bore his flamboyant coat of arms, with the unconvincing motto *"Crede Byron"*-Believe in Byron.

In Belgium he stopped off at the field of Waterloo to see where his hero Napoleon had battled it out against Wellington thee years earlier. He was often compared with the little Corsican, whose defeat he felt sorry for.

They passed through Luxembourg, and then followed the Rhine down to Switzerland. He was chasing his latest mistress Theresa, and her husband Count Guccioli, to Ravenna.

He was also following in the footsteps of his friend "the notorious atheist Mr Shelley who had been expelled from just about everywhere." Worse still, "he was a man who was sharing 'promiscuous intercourse' with two sisters, and was generally embroiled in 'a satanic league of incestuous relationships'. So went the gossip that travelled back to London from Tuscany.

'Incest is a very poetical circumstance', Shelley once justified in a letter.

Percy and Mary Shelley, with Claire Claremont, had decided to spend the winter in Pisa on the other side of the Italian peninsula, in their own threesome.

Meanwhile Gordon was ensconced in his own convenient, though not always friendly, *Menagerie* with the young Theresa and her husband Count Guiccioli. Theresa's father and brother were both involved in a quasi Masonic group with the aim of ridding Italy of the Austrians and of improving the country's morals. This appealed to Gordon's schemes and dreams. When it became clear that the Count and his family had to flee into exile from the clutches of the Venetian Republic, Gordon suggested that rather than escape to Switzerland, why not move across to Pisa? The Dukedom of Tuscany, then under Austrian rule, was less than a hundred miles away as the crow flies. There they could join forces and make up a group, with his friend Percy and Mary and his ex girlfriend Claire, in the opulent style to which Gordon was accustomed. His poor little Allegra, aged 5, was packed off to a convent.

Gordon set forth in his usual extravagant style with his zoological companions. The birds were caged up, next to the monkeys and the wolves. The dogs ran alongside the carriages.

The cavalcade which advanced included the seven servants accompanying the five coaches which had travelled all the way from England. It swept along the road from Ravenna, in clouds of dust, and a cacophony of animal sounds – squawking, screeching, yelping and baying. They drove all and sundry into the ditches - the plebs and contadini, as well as the great and good, who, in all manner of public and private coaches, were creaming along this torturous, narrow highway over the mountains into the heart of Tuscany.

When the procession reached Florence, every window was flung open, and every tourist gawked to see the dissolute 'Milord Inglese' step out in style. His fame had spread before him. Having checked in at the hotel, it was a toss-up to see whether he would be up to his usual tricks, i.e. getting his Lordships' lusty leg over the nearest available maid - as he had done on arrival in France from England. He bragged that he mixed with all classes, from the *conte* to the *contadino*.

There were too many tourists in Florence, so they decided to move on. The procession advanced, following the well worn route along the banks of the Arno River to Pisa.

They passed the village of Vinci, birthplace of Leonardo, and the little town of San Miniato, birthplace of the Grand Countess Matilda di Canossa, whose far reaching influence as a woman of great strength of character, combined beauty and brains with enormous influence throughout Tuscany. Such was her stature and fame that even the great Michelangelo Buonarotti claimed to be related to her.

Gordon eventually arrived at his rented Palazzo Lanfranchi, a rambling pile of opulent rooms overlooking the banks of the Arno, in the middle of the city.

The seven servants took stock. The hens and horses were stabled behind. The dogs were left to roam around the building. The furniture was unloaded, including the billiard table, and Gordon's vast library of books, as well as a selection of French Empire furniture and drapes. Everything was dragged up to the *Piano Nobile* (the First Floor) via the ornate marble staircase

– the design of which Gordon credited to Michelangelo.

The echoing top floor rooms below the eaves were apparently haunted. The massive underground cellars, below the river's waterline, were permanently damp. Occasionally, Gordon was inspired to spend the night there to get away from the spooks. His valet also insisted on moving rooms immediately because of the poltergeists. So the top floor was left more or less empty. Having been brought up in a strong Calvinistic upbringing in Aberdeen, Gordon was reluctant to call in a Catholic priest to exorcise these demons, or lay to rest these poor lost souls. It was against his better judgment, and he considered it the last resort. The Presbyterian influence of his mother, who hailed from a mad line of the Gordon Clan and the early experience of a frightful Scottish nurse, had bred an air of gloom, despondency and mistrust in all things spiritual. Not to mention devilishness. Yet he was inspired by all this fatalism. In contrast to the strict Calvinism of his youth, Roman Catholicism appealed to him as a natural successor. He regarded it as the greatest of all the branches of Christianity, to be modified with a certain amount of licence. The theatrical and therapeutic side of the "smells, bells and yells" stimulated his senses, and he searched for the divine in the sexual.

'Religion is about life, and sexuality is the fountain of life,' he declared.

No sooner had he settled in, than from across the River Arno, a high pitched shout was heard. It heralded the arrival of the atheist Percy Shelley – 'an angel touched by lunacy'. He was in one of his reckless moods of creative energy.

Conveniently, the Shelley's had chosen apartments on the other side of the waterway, almost directly opposite, in one of the *Tre Palazzi di Chiesa* - The Three Church Palaces.

The Arno was awash with sundry boats sailing to and from Pisa, Florence and the sea. This sluggish waterway was fed from the malaria infested marshes of the Maremma on one side, and a labyrinth of canals which stretched through the lush flat lands, joining the Serchio River from Lucca, with the Arno.

The bridges of the city were well spaced apart, and the centre of Pisa lay at the heart of the sweeping waterway. Along the river banks nestled craft crammed with produce: fish, fruit, and vegetables, as well as a few dilapidated sailing dinghies. However, for a City which was the seat of power of the Grand Duke of Tuscany, and also boasted a University specialising in the Sciences since before the days of Galileo, Pisa was under populated. It was indeed 'Pisa pining over her desert stream.'

The Shelley's more modest rented pile had separate apartments for themselves and their friends the Williams', who had also travelled out from England.

Edward Williams was a part time cavalry officer and aspiring writer who had lost his money in Madras with a bank that went bust. He had brought out his girlfriend Jane, the wife of a fellow naval officer, who had been married at sixteen and had been beaten up by her husband in India. She had escaped back to England, and disappeared with Williams without waiting for a divorce. Jane was highly attractive and musical. Also hanging around were a couple of other aspiring scribblers of 'Little Tuscany' - hoping to get into print.

Most mysterious of all was Edward Trelawny, who was a far cry from the others. He was a side kick of the Williams' who had travelled out to shoot wild fowl in the nearby Maremma marshes. To have called him a free-booter would have been kind. Colourful, cunning and hawkish, with Moorish looks and a dark beard, this randy Cornish rogue had also deserted the British Navy in India after beating up an officer, joined some French mercenaries, and had eventually slipped back into England. His manners were wilder than his imagination - which was boundless. Fact blended with fiction, and he left a trail of half truths, embellishments and downright lies. Yet this swashbuckling 'con-man' was utterly devoted to, and simply infatuated with Percy's weak character, flitting ways and misunderstood genius.

Trelawny very soon went across the river to arrange a meeting with the equally flippant man of the world, Gordon Byron. Not for nothing did Gordon call Percy 'The Snake' - a reference to his quick wit and nervous movements.

At the Palazzo Lanfranchi on Wednesday evenings wild dinners were the order of the evening. The Pistol Club was a male only affair started by Gordon, to encourage the increasing circle of British exiles to drop in, and make useful contacts with the local *Literati, Glitterati* and *Eminenti,* as well as meet the other Regency fops who had travelled out to Italy to escape what Gordon aptly described: 'The English winter - ending in July, to recommence in August'.

Pistol Club dinners sometimes went on untill 3 in the morning, during which large quantities of claret were consumed. The boisterous discussions centred on philosophy, verse and impromptu theatricals. The host had a habit of closing his eyes and falling asleep, only to wake up suddenly with such witty and endearing ejaculations as: 'Sweet is revenge, especially to women", and: 'Pleasure is a Sin, and sometimes Sin's a pleasure'. Or 'What men call gallantry and the God's adultery is much more common when the weather's sultry'.

He would seize a brandy glass in one hand and his sword stick in the other, and swagger around the dining room table singing his own vulgar version of an aria by Rossini. Then just as suddenly he would sit down and carry on the conversation until the wee hours. A visitor described it:

"Like other parties of the kind, it was first silent, then talky, them argumentative, then disputatious, then unintelligible, then altogether, then inarticulate, then drunk".

The erratic Percy would arrive, wide eyed and tousled haired, carelessly dressed with gravy stains and buttons missing. In contrast to Gordon's compact stature he was tall and stooping. Wild, reckless and sensitive, he was also bashful and shy.

Although Vulgar was the word for many of the attitudes of his friends, Percy's manners were immaculate He was a born gentleman, although defiantly eccentric: He was appalled by tacky Italian habits: "What do you think? Young women of rank actually eat – you will never guess what – Garlic!"

No doubt he was aware of the old Roman saying of Marcus Martialis in AD 100: 'He who bears chives on his breath is safe from being kissed to death.'

Gordon appreciated his *savoir faire*. He copied him, since his own Scottish mother, had failed him.

This little nest of singing birds was joined by the ravishingly beautiful Cornelia de Boinville, and her equally tasty mother, whose family connections included one of Napoleon's Generals This sexually liberated society, real and imagined, included two of Percy's most stoical friends - the warm-hearted Leigh Hunt, and his cousin and schoolmate, Thomas Medwin.

Count Taafe, was an eccentric Irishman whose improvised poetical contribution amused everyone. Then there was Pacchiani, a dubious Professor at Pisa University, who made himself useful by introducing the Shelleys to the local nobility. This included Emilia Viviani, the ravishingly beautiful 19 year old daughter of the Governor of Pisa. She had been relegated to a convent, and was about to be sent off to an arranged marriage with an Italian nobleman. When Percy set eyes on this stunning adolescent angel, he was mesmerised into using her as the model for countless stanzas. She was the personification of his boundless lyrical belief in the power of human love, which he immortalised in some of his verse. He dreamed of her, and longed for her as a twin sister, alongside his wife. Their intense whirlwind romance and strong physical bond with each other was conveniently overlooked by the long suffering Mary. He liked Emilia to cross dress in boys clothing, since she was like a Greek Goddess of doubtful gender. 'Heavenly Hermaphrodite, sweet marble monster of both sexes'. Her bold sparkling lasciviousness and ambi-dextrous behaviour was the scandal of Pisa at the time, especially since she was the daughter of the Governor.

*Over half a century later, in Victorian times, when Emilia (Viviani) had finally escaped from her hapless marriage, Shelley's old cousin Tom Medwin visited her in Florence shortly before her death. He wrote: "I might fill many a page, by speaking of the tears she shed over the memory of Shelley."*

The only one missing was Keats. He would hardly have fitted in with this miscellany of madness. Byron considered him "a miserable self-polluter of the human mind," who wrote 'drivel'.

It was Shelley who first met Keats, and shaped the poet's destiny. He helped him publish his first book of verse and invited him to Italy. Keats turned the offer down, but a year later arrived in Rome. Two years later he was dead.

"When is your little daughter Allegra arriving in Pisa?" Byron was constantly asked.

"I have packed her off to the good nuns in the convent."

Not a year later she caught a virus and died. Thus went to Heaven the third of his daughters. After Allegra's death, the volatile, moody Clare never forgave poor Mary for being friends with Byron. Naturally, she excused Percy, her equally infatuated lover.

"The more lovers a woman takes, the more

powerful her sense of liberation" was the philosophy of this sexually liberated society.

Pisa at that time was the height of decadent society. The mild, short winters brought about only four months of raw weather. With the Grand Duke of Tuscany in residence for the winter season, it was a robust round of balls and parties. The narrow streets were crammed with carriages, and people carried in *chaise longues*. It was probably the most swinging place in all Italy, with its crowd of young *Belezzas* and *Magnificos*. Florence, by comparison - in spite of its unparalleled artistic position in Europe, was dowdy.

Gordon made himself known to the authorities in no uncertain terms. His Republican views had followed him across Europe. There were spies everywhere. The head of the Intelligence Service of the day, the *'Spia delle Spie'* (Spy of all spies), Cavalliere Luigi Tonelli, who reported directly to the occupying Austrian authorities, commented:

"The famous poet Lord Byron, who, if he had not the reputation of being mad, ought to be watched by all the police forces of Europe. He has taken the Palazzo Lanfranchi, for a year, at a rent of 200 zecchini, paying 6 months in advance."

Although his servants had been involved in a skirmish with some dragoons, the English community rallied to Byrons support. Due to his rank and international fame, there was little that the occupying Austrian or the Papal authorities could do about him. Instead they hounded the Guicciolis from pillar to post, driving the Count altogether out of Tuscany. Meanwhile Theresa gave them the slip and stayed on.

Shelley, physically weak and spiritually lonely, would slink off with Edwards Williams to sail on the Arno in a light skiff, or join in Byron's pistol practice. Both Percy and Gordon preferred night to day. They would get up late. After brunch, they rapped away till late afternoon, when they would get on their horses and gallop off into the woods and pine forests just outside the walls of Pisa, towards the sea. Before darkness set in they would dismount and then pistol practice at pumpkin targets in the woods. Both were good shots. Sometimes Percy sat near the mouth of the Arno where the revolutionary poet turned his attention to the lyrical. Here he composed some of the saddest and sweetest verse during the winter of 1821 - 1822, dedicated to his chum Williams' tender hearted wife Jane.

It was Trelawney who fatally introduced Percy to water, and tried to teach him to swim. He found a deep pool in the Arno and told him to jump in. He did so, sunk straight to the bottom and lay there. If it had not been for the young rogue jumping in and rescuing him, he would have drowned. "Truth lies in the bottom of the well - I'll find it," Percy shouted, "Don't tell Mary though - not a word!"

On another occasion, Mary and Trelawney went looking for Percy, who had wandered off into the depths of the Cascine pine forest which stretched down to the sea. She gave up the search, whilst Trelawney continued. Eventually he came across an old woodsman who said *"Vieni qui"*. He would show him where the *Pazzo Inglese* 'the Mad Englishman' was hidden. Not surprisingly, beside a pool of water, they came across scattered books and loose papers, with fragments of verse. *"Ecco lo!"* cried the woodsman. Trelawney half expected to see him lying beneath the water. He emerged from the shadows of a fallen tree trunk, and once again exclaimed: "Poor Mary, Don't tell her."

I waited for Inge and Angela to arrive by train from England. The night sleeper from Paris pulled in exactly on time at the utilitarian Pisa Central Station.

When the railways arrived in the 1850's, they developed slowly and separately on an individual basis - fiefdom by fiefdom. Kingdoms, Grand Duchy's and Principalities went their separate ways, and so, unlike the rest of Europe, the railways played little part in unifying the country till later - apart from Cavour's memorable line in 1854 which linked Turin with Genoa. Until the unification of Italy in the 1860's and 1870's over 60 per cent of the coal used by steam locomotives was imported from Britain. During those years over half the spending on the country's infrastructure went on railways.

As we walked along the banks of the Arno we passed Byron's old haunted hangout the Palazzo Lanfranchi - now the Palazzo Toscanelli.

"Look here - Tuscany under Austrian rule" Inge mused. We had reached the Grand Hotel Victoria, with its air of detached nostalgia on the Lungarno, and were admiring a parchment scroll on the wall. It proclaimed: 'Leopold the Second, by the Grace of God, Prince Imperial of Austria, Royal Prince of Hungary and Bohemia and Grand Duke of Tuscany'.

"Can't imagine what the locals thought."

The Hotel is still run by the same family that

have owned it for six generations. Four hundred years ago the original Tavern had been named the *Locanda della Vittoria*, when the victorious Florentines celebrated their takeover of Pisa. In the 1830's a local Luccan, Pasquale Piegaja was working in London, organising Grand Tours to Tuscany, and renting out villas to the prosperous English of the day. He returned to Pisa with even grander ideas, and purchased an adjoining old palace with a group of ancient ruins and towers. In 1839 the new hotel opened its doors. The name was changed during Victorian times to the anglicised Hotel Victoria. It developed into Pisa's first proper hotel with modern facilities purposely designed for the visiting English gentry on their Grand Tour.

This was an English invention, first coined by Richard Lassells in his 1670 book 'Voyage to Italy'. The Grand Tour developed into a cultural experience *par excellence* for the rich young blades of the day who were expecting an inheritance. It was not just a bronzed and breezy jaunt to Italy to discover the treasures of art and architecture in Florence, Rome and Milan. Their aim was to spend months on end in various alluring haunts of culture and revelry, notably the great Italian cities.

A trip through France brought the flesh-pots of Paris, and a trip down the Rhine through Bavaria included the Swiss Lakes and mountains. Often lasting the best part of a year, they were sometimes accompanied by their girlfriends or wives. They sauntered through the continent on the well-worn route of good roads *via* France or the Low Countries, then over the Alps from Switzerland. If the roads were impassable, their carriages were sometimes taken to pieces, and carried across. Passengers went on foot, or by sedan chair. 6, 8 or even 10 chairmen were employed to carry each person, dependant upon their weight. Mules carried the servants, baggage and parts of a coach. At 2 shillings and sixpence, the fee for a chairman or a mule was the same. This arduous trip was expensive and dangerous, with bad Inns and grubby lodgings. Brigands and robbers abounded. The most favoured way from Geneva or Lyon was over the Mont Cenis Pass to Turin. Other trickier alpine passes were used, like the Brenner and St.Bernhard.

The alternative route from England was by sea to a French port such as Marseille, (or overland from Lyon to Marseille) from where the final landing was at Genoa, or Leghorn - the nearest port to Pisa and Florence. Leghorn (Livorno) was the favoured stopping point, nourished by a flourishing English community. It was a short distance to Pisa. Encouraged by the Romantic poets, 'Grand Tourists' began to spend winter in Pisa, attracted by the mild climate and low prices. It was possible to rent a finely furnished villa or *palazzo*, with stabling for horses, and employ many servants, for about a third of what it would cost in England. Florence was the other gem in Tuscany. The tight community of insular English expatriates had their own Anglican church, graveyard, chemist and grocery shop. The *Inglese* were later joined by *Americani* of similar ilk. Of all the hostelries in Florence, the most exclusive was Schneider's Hotel on the north bank of the Arno. It was known as the *Locanda d'Inghilterra* or the Arms of England.

Armed with letters of introduction, the 'Grand Tourists' would often overcrowd the villas of their country's Envoys and Consuls; or rent apartments 'for the duration' using letters of credit from their banks in England.

For the blue blooded revellers, drinking, gambling, and cavorting with well heeled countesses and courtesans was the usual bill of fare. Added temptations included all manner of dubious vices such as the cross-dressed pretty boys of Florence, as well as the services of an occasional naughty novice nun in an accommodating convent.

Although Rome was the usual southern most limit, Venice was the jewel of the Grand Tour, until the opening up of Pompeii and Herculaneum in the mid 1700's. The Bay of Naples – 'a pearl in its lustrous shell' then became the big attraction. It took 4 to 5 days to travel the 150 miles from Rome to Naples, on appalling roads at less than 3 miles an hour, whilst taking pot-luck in overnight *osterias.*

For a time, an added attraction in Naples was Emma Hamilton, wife of Sir William, the British Minister to the Neapolitan Court. As Nelsons' girlfriend, she attracted as much, if not more attention than Vesuvius itself. Sophisticated travellers, who would normally have disdained her unpolished company, made a point of calling on this flamboyant hostess.

The chronicler McCauley noted that as the Railways extended further and further into Europe, the Grand Tour 'as an object in itself will disappear.' The Mont Cenis railway tunnel between France and Italy was started in 1857, and finally did away with the need to cross the Alps on foot or in a sedan chair or rickety carriage.

Not far from Pisa's main Railway Station, we sat in the historic Leopolda Restaurant in the original station - now a nice old national monument. It had been built as part of the Austro-Hungarian Emperor and Grand Duke Leopold's ambitious plan to link Livorno with Florence. The British engineer Robert Stephenson had convinced the Grand Duke that a link through Pisa would be the most economically viable way from the coast to the heart of Tuscany.

The first stretch of the 'Leopolda' line between Livorno and Pisa took 3 years to build.

The modest beginning of Pisa's arch roofed station with two platforms - one for passengers and one for goods - was soon overtaken by events. Within 20 years a bigger new terminus was constructed nearer the centre of town.

At the next table to us was an aged white haired professor with a rather studious girl in glasses. We got talking. He had been visiting his daughter at Pisa University and was returning to Rome. He turned to my two companions.

"Are you travelling to Rome?" he asked.

"No. We're going to Lucca; then up through the mountains, round and down to the sea. Then back to Pisa again along the coast. It's a kind of poetic pilgrimage. We shall stop on the way and explore as we go."

"Not like the Rome Express," he replied.

"That train up the mountains is simple and slow, and the railway is one of the most under used in Italy," he commented.

"Once upon a time it made the whole area rich. Modern transport was the key to our prosperity. Now the big lorries come thundering down, across the mountains. They have no time to stop. Only passengers use that railway."

**'A man who has not been to Italy is always conscious of his inferiority'**.

Samuel Johnson

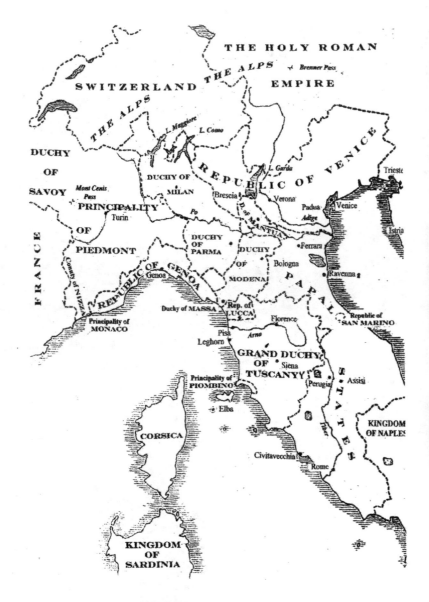

**_ITALY IN THE 1700's_**

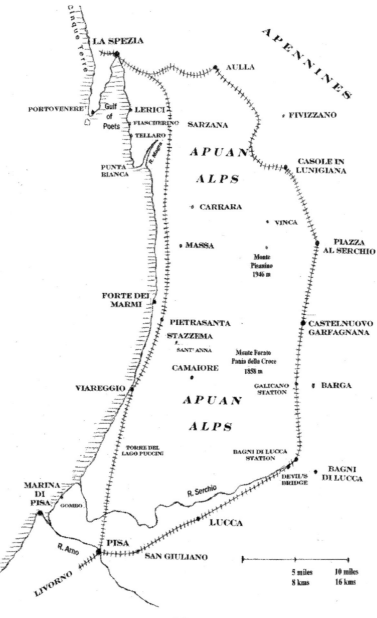

CINQUE TERRE

LA SPEZIA

AULLA

APENNINES

PORTOVENERE

Gulf of Poets

LERICI

FIASCHERINO

SARZANA

TELLARO

FIVIZZANO

PUNTA BIANCA

R. Magra

APUAN

ALPS

CASOLE IN LUNIGIANA

CARRARA

VINCA

MASSA

Monte Pisanino 1946 m

PIAZZA AL SERCHIO

FORTE DEI MARMI

PIETRASANTA

STAZZEMA

SANT' ANNA

CAMAIORE

Monte Forato Pania della Croce 1858 m

CASTELNUOVO GARFAGNANA

VIAREGGIO

APUAN

ALPS

GALICANO STATION

BARGA

TORRE DEL LAGO PUCCINI

BAGNI DI LUCCA STATION

BAGNI DI LUCCA

MARINA DI PISA

GOMBO

R. Serchio

DEVIL'S BRIDGE

PISA

LUCCA

R. Arno

SAN GIULIANO

LIVORNO

5 miles    10 miles
8 kms    16 kms

# Chapter 2

## LUCCA

~~~

With a backdrop of the Apuan Alps, Pisa's open plains - facing the sea - are criss-crossed with hidden ditches and weedy canals. Beneath the steep hillside stands the elegant little Spa village of San Giuliano. It is half way between Pisa and Lucca, joined by a pass in the wooded hills which once separated these two warring cities. The thermal Baths nestle under the cliffs, raggedly scarred by rude remnants of earlier quarrying efforts to extract indifferent marble.

The three of us hopped off the train at San Giuliano Terme Station, walked a few blocks, and booked into the nearby Pensione, opposite the house in the Piazza where the Shelley's had once stayed. A plaque on the wall outside records their sojourn: 'In 1820 and 1821 the poet Percy Bysshe Shelley, in the purity of the Tuscan countryside, created his masterpiece Adonais'. This was his great elegy to John Keats, with a tantalising prophecy of his own death.

Mary Shelley had been eager to escape from Pisa, with the gossip and prying eyes of the English expatriate community, who looked down on her as a liberal girl from a trendy background who had run off with a married man, and borne his children illegitimately.

So they moved into this house on the banks of the stream in the middle of San Giuliano. The frontage looked out towards the baths, and the wooded slopes leading up to the towering slopes of the mountain. Here, according to the locals, numerous small caves and grottoes hid Witches, Fairies and Hobgoblins. The back of the house faced a small garden along the banks of the canal, a slow running waterway which ran into the flatlands surrounding the town.

Mary recalled: "Our stay at the Baths of San Giuliano were shortened by an accident. At the foot of our garden ran the canal which ran between the Serchio and the Arno. The Serchio overflowed its banks, and the canal also overflowed. As this part of the country is below the river level, it was quickly flooded. The rising waters filled the square of the Baths, in the lower part of which our house was situated. The canal overflowed in the garden behind us, and the rising waters burst open the doors and rose to a height of six feet.

"There were no pleasure boats on the Arno. However Percy overcame this difficulty. With a friend, he constructed a boat like the huntsmen carry about with them in the Maremma. It was a lightweight boat of laths and pitched canvas, designed to cross the sluggish streams that cross the forests, and join the Serchio with the Arno. The locals, who remonstrated on the danger, could not understand how anyone could take pleasure in an exercise that risked life. *'Ma va per la vita!'* they exclaimed, 'Go for your life!'

Percy, however, pined for the wide open sea. Mary recalled: "He wished that our summers, instead of being passed among the hills near Pisa, should be spent on the shores of the sea. It was difficult to find a spot. Leghorn had lost its only attraction, since our friends had returned to England; and, Montenero (outside Leghorn) being the resort of many English, we did not wish to find ourselves in a colony of chance travellers.

"The low lands and bad air of the Maremma stretch the whole length of the western shores till broken by the rocks and hills of La Spezia. It was a vague idea, but Percy suggested an excursion to see whether it would be feasible to spend the summer there."

The Maremma was a mozzy infested swamp that kept people at bay. *Mal Aria* - Bad Air – had caused havoc through the centuries. Some say it was one of the causes of the fall of the Roman Empire – along with homosexuality and an infusion of foreigners. The swamp was only drained much later; and the effects of the mosquito still linger on.

Through the pass from the Baths of Sam Guiliano we were back on track. One of the earliest railways in Italy, the line was built in the 1850's by the Grand Duke of Tuscany, to link Pisa with Lucca. The idea was to exactly copy King Ferdinand of Naples, who had constructed the first 'Italian Peninsula' railway line in his Kingdom of Two Sicilies in 1839. It linked his Neapolitan Palace with his Summer Palace at Portico, just 7 kilometres away. The line was extended further along the spectacular Bay of Naples joining the little villages under Mount Vesuvius. Designed by a Frenchman, it was constructed by Italians. The first 3 locomotives - which ran on imported British coal – were supplied by Longridge & Co of Northumberland. [1]

*It was built only 9 years after Britain's first real metropolitan railway line linking Liverpool with Manchester was opened in 1830 - fifteen years after the Battle of Waterloo.*

We hugged the mountains and trundled past Ripafratta, the shadowy town of dingy narrow streets, whose only light came at sunset from the west. Here the road, railway and the river run in tandem through the narrow gorge – so close you can almost touch the passing cars and trains.

We arrived at Lucca, the stoutly barricaded city of many towers and squares. Sane, civilized and cosy. The working Italian town that is the only large city still totally enclosed by walls.

"Lucca - the neatest, the regularist, the exactest, the most fly-in-amber little town in the world. With its uncrowded streets", wrote Evelyn Waugh.

When the French invaded Lucca in 1805-1806 they carried off everything they could, and the Emperor Napoleon installed his sister Elisa as Princess in command of the Duchy of Lucca.. She had married an Italian Prince. Most of the country was handed over to the Austrians. The locals went berserk.

Addressing a crowd of incensed Italians who had been robbed of their birthright, the little Corsican Napoleon Buonaparte, born a Genoese, shouted at them:

*'Gli Italiani tutti ladroni'*. - "Italians are all Robbers!"

*'Non tutti ma **buona parte**'*. – "Not all but for the most part!" shouted back one brave lady in the crowd.

Another local grandee described the Corsican to his wife: "He was so small and skinny and dishevelled, that at first glance he looked like a boy-man, a strangely magnetic creature, very youthful yet astonishingly self assured".

Ten years later, the Congress of Vienna was in full swing. It had opened officially as a series of international diplomatic councils ever since Napoleon had been defeated in Russia, and had escaped from exile to meet his Waterloo in 1815. The great powers were busy carving up Europe for themselves. Francis, the Emperor of Austria was in the chair. Britain, Russia and Prussia were hovering in the wings, whilst France was altogether sidelined. All of a sudden, tiny Lucca appeared on the scene. This rich little independent Republic added a tender request for its independence from Austrian clutches. However the Emperor Francis was keen to hang on to this precious little City-State in the middle of Tuscany - the rest of which he controlled. He answered Lucca in pontifical terms "Everyone is hungry, and I need to eat too. It better that **I** should eat **you** than another." [2]

It was to be another 30 to 40 years before Italy was finally unified, and the Austrians departed. The Railways played a key role in this. King Victor Emmanuel of Savoy, Piedmont, and Sardinia wooed Napoleon III of France, who was Buonaparte's nephew to help drive the Austrians out of northern Italy. Troops were speedily entrained from all over France and shipped from Marseille to the port of Genoa; thence on to Alessandria by train. Without the benefit of the railway, the Austrians were out of touch and ran short of supplies. They were finally defeated near Lake Garda. As a reward for Napoleons help, the territory of Savoy was given to France.

Reclusive little Lucca is a bicyclists paradise - at the same time a pedestrians dream. No longer do cars drive around the top of the wide tree lined walls. Elegant and easy-going, the town is dominated by a tall Clock Tower, from the top of which sprout ancient oak trees. There were once 130 towers all sprouting holm oaks. Now, only one is left. It was not pulled down to build the Fortress with its stone, but because it was the only tower left with a working clock.

We passed the antique restaurant that had been established in 1782, some 30 years before Byron and Shelley were here.

Across the way lay the Church of Lucca's patron saint. Saint Frediano, the local Italian bishop, was in fact a canny Irish monk. Son of King Ultach of Ulster, he then became a priest. Around 565 AD he went on a pilgrimage to visit the Pope, taking the ancient route connecting Canterbury to Rome. This was the Via Francigena. The pilgrims crossed the English Channel, and passed from Calais through Reims, over the St Bernhard Pass to Aosta, then through Pavia and Pontremoli. Then they turned towards the coast, past Luni and Massa, From Pietrasanta they swerved inland to Camaiore. Then the pilgrims reached Lucca.

Gazing up at the mountains as they travelled along the coast, Saint Freddy liked the look of the lofty Monte Pisano, which stood out for miles around. So he decided to become a meditating Hermit on the Hill, and confront the Devil. Such was his fame, far and wide, that the Pope persuaded him to come down and become Bishop of Lucca.

Apart from his confrontations with the devil, he is famed for an even more fanciful achievement. The River Serchio overflowed its banks. It washed right up to the walls of Lucca, threatening the city. The locals called for their bishop. Freddy called for an ordinary rake, and proceeded to trace a new course for the River Serchio to follow, avoiding the cultivated lands around the city. Miraculously, the river followed his bearings.

In San Frediano's Church lies the body of St. Richard, another Anglo-Saxon saint. Nearby lies the body of Saint Zita, the patron saint of waitresses and chambermaids. She was the honest and industrious local *domestico* who won over the other skiving household workers with her patience and humility.

*Per San Fred la neve al monte e al piano.*

For Saint Fred's feast day, there's snow on the mountains and on the plains below. Goes another saying: Old women's teeth rattle on the feast of San Frediano, at the end of November.

Everything in peaceful Lucca is at ease and at rest under the sun. Its walls kept intact for 500 years an independent republic. The Silk trade flourished, so they took over Carrara, and became rich on its marble. Lucca's Balducci Bank was the only one in the area to pay for Michelangelo's marble, since neither Massa nor Carrara had banks.

It is as sharp and trim as its own map. Many corners and alleyways ring to the sounds of Puccini. He was born and brought up within its walls, where he eventually made his fortune.

Giacomo Antonio Domenico Michele Secondo Maria Puccini was the fifth of 7 children in 5 generations of Italian musicians. To begin with he showed no interest in music. However, a visit to Pisa to see Verdi's Aida spurred him into action. He was destined thereafter to follow in his footsteps

"God touched me with his little fingers and said: Write for the theatre, only the theatre!"

He studied music with his uncle, who kept Lucca Cathedral's organ seat warm for his nephew. He learned the hard and interesting way, singing in the choir, and playing music to the nuns in the convent - as well as to the girls in the local brothel. He also worked part time in the Casino. At one time he was so hard up that he stole the organ pipes from a nearby village church to pay for his wild fowl shooting. Later he purchased an estate at Torre del Lago, on Lake Massaciucoli, near the sea, where he collected racing cars, and enjoyed other wild sporting habits. He overcame his melancholia by relief in violent sex, shooting birds and driving high powered racing cars at reckless speed. Often short of the right story line for his musical compositions, he bragged: "I am almost always in love. I am a mighty hunter of Wild fowl, beautiful Women and Opera Libretti" He pressed his song-smiths to produce "a libretto that would move the world". One came up with the idea of Dickens' Oliver Twist.

We sat in Lucca's favourite old Antico Caffe Sino, where Puccini spent his afternoons. And we ate Puccini's favourite wildfowl dish which he had created called *Folaghe alla Puccini*, Coot alla Puccini. He had specially created this for his 'Club de La Boheme' at Torre del Lago - to glorify not just the success of his 'Bohemian' opera - but to celebrate the sins of gluttony and intemperance. And we drank St Torpes, a white wine that has been produced since AD 100 in the Pisan hills south of Lucca. It was named after Saint Torpes, a valiant Roman centurion who was beheaded by Nero. Legend tells of his body, abandoned in a boat, drifted across the sea to the coast of France, and landed at a place which was named in his honour St. Tropez.

Wines thrive in the foothills of Apennines. Halfway between Lucca and Montecatini lies the wine city of Montecarlo. It was once on the Roman Wine Route across the mountains when it was called the Via Vinaia. A small town with a miraculous theatre - *Teatro dei Rassicuranti* – it has superb views across the plains.

A favourite of the Renaissance Popes and the Medicis, the local Montecarlo wine was made from grapes imported from France. It was christened *Lo Chablis di Montecarlo*. Dozens of cases were sent down the line and drunk at the wedding of King Umberto II in 1930.

The canny wine makers now rely on their play of words to make a chink in the oriental curtain. They export loads of Montecarlo wine to China, where the Asian wine *fundis* are fooled into thinking it comes from Monte Carlo proper - its more famous pricey namesake on the French Riviera.

Nearby Montecatini is the spa town with 'Liberty Style' Art Nouveau villas. In its heyday of elegance, from 1898 onwards, Verdi spent nineteen consecutive summers here immersed in the flamboyant architecture, open gardens, wide avenues and vaporous waters.  It was a magnet which attracted all the great composers of the day – including Puccini, Rossini, Mascagni, Strauss and Caruso himself.

"You may have the universe if I may have Italy" declared Verdi.

After lunch we snoozed on the grassy ramparts of Lucca, this docile Tuscan city of music and mountains, unadulterated by tourists.

**"You view from afar the grey olive trees**
**Misty in the rain;**
**or the Serchio river and woodlands**
**which encircle the city"** [3]

Gabriele D'Annunzio

The three of us walked eagerly to the railway station, through the deep and cavernous walls. We were confronted by what looked like a dead end, but we found a gap in the ramparts with electric light illuminating a long narrow stretch.

Plastered all over the place was: I LOVE YOU LUCCA

In measured melodious tones of Italian, and then English, every train was greeted in and out of the station, as we waited for our trip up the mountains.

---

[1]  Quoted in **Blood, Iron & Gold** by Christian Wolmar
[2]  Quoted in **Rites of Peace** by Adam Zamoyski
[3]  Gabriele D'Annunzio – Lauds – Electra – Lucca

# Chapter 3

# THE BATHS OF LUCCA

~~~~

The train departed with a timely jolt. It rattled out through the extremities of lovely smiling Lucca - peaceful, prosperous and content. The railway line follows the Serchio River valley to where it breaks through the hills that form an almost complete barrier around the city. Diesel engines ensure no overhead wires mar the landscape, as we rumble past small fertile cornfields, almond and olive plantations. Within a few minutes, the foothills of the Apennines are spread before us.

*'And the red and golden vines, piercing with their trellised lines, the olive-sandaled Apennines'* [1]

In the distance, the highest peaks are clouded over. They still hold their winter snow till long after spring has arrived.

We rattle and clank our way alongside the river, flowing swiftly in places, and then sometimes lapping against sandy or pebbly coves. Once upon a time it was a wide waterway, navigable the whole way through. Flowing round Lucca, it gapped the wooded hills, onto the open plain towards the sea, where it stole the heart of the impetuous Percy Shelley.

*'Our boat is asleep on Serchio's stream; its sails are folded like thoughts in a dream'* [2]

A jet-stream of lorries zaps across a spectacular new concrete bridge. Far below us, the harvest that used to be carried on the backs of donkeys in huge baskets is now being pulled on the backs of tiny buzzing *Apis*.

These little Vespa tractors buzz like bees all over Italy, and keep the rural economy flourishing. A flock of goats is grazing down by the water's edge, unruffled by the noise. A horse is munching a mouthful, and an old woman is standing at the edge of the turbulent current.

Our train whines into a tunnel through the escarpment, and dives out the other side, straight as a die, over a rattling old railway bridge, strutting across the river. Beside us lies another stunning old masterpiece; a narrow bridge of stone so elegantly camel-arched that even the Devil couldn't break its back. From both sides you stagger up the steep incline to the middle, and you roll down the other side. Like a prone lady stretching her back towards heaven, or a giant Ace of Spades, its lofty mid-centre is arched high enough to allow the tallest ships to sail along the river. The bridge was built by the local structural engineers 400 years ago, for the far-sighted Countess Matilda of Tuscany, who combined beauty and brains with awesome energy. She wanted a quick way across the dodgy river to reach the healthy spa waters of *Bagni di Lucca* – The Baths of Lucca.

Unfortunately, the superstitious stone masons fell badly behind schedule, and so, they came to confront the Devil himself. On the advice of the Bishop of Lucca, St. Frediano, the canny Irishman, they made a pact with Satan. "Leave the rest of us alone in this Paradise on Earth", they said, "and you can have the soul of the first one over our completed bridge". The scheming locals proved their point. When the time came to cross the bridge, they sent over a Pig. The devil disappeared into the depths of the river, his tail between his legs - robbed of his dream for all eternity.

We hurry past old fortifications in the mountain side. A pock-marked wall is inscribed in large letters: 'Fortifications of the Gothic Line'. This shell-shocked reminder of the Second World War was built largely with forced labour. It was the last stand of the retreating Germans and it sliced right across Italy, through the spine of the Apennines. Paradoxically, the Germans named it after the Byzantines who had used this same, age-old mountain barrier to prevent the hordes of Goths from sweeping down from the north.

We rattle into the station of Bagni di Lucca. Marble statues of nubile nymphs adorn each end of the rough old platform. These classic figures, in scanty togas, look as if they've been stuck on display for 'cultural correctness'. The one eyed virgin, or cock-eyed Venus, has a broken nose. The private parts of Bacchus have taken a beating. Aerosol paint has been in action on the Goddess of Love and the God of Wine.

The train waited. Silence reigned on the dreary platform. Someone cleared his throat. The colourful stationmaster appeared in a bright red cap, trimmed with gold. He flourished a green flag, and pursed his lips, imperiously, over a large silver whistle. With these politically correct colours, he made a sort of Palio flirtation, and signalled the train's departure with a shrill blast. It was a patriotic gesture which combined well with the romance of this Edwardian era railway, which finally arrived here from Lucca just before the First World War.

Like many remote rail stations in Italy, the name on the platform has no proximity to the town. It is 3 miles from Bagni di Lucca; so we bus along the narrow road, lined with cypress trees. We pass the Casino, one of the oldest in Europe, where roulette was first played. Until recently it was the headquarters of a fringe crowd of docile religious fanatics. Now it has reopened with a fanfare of fruit machines.

In the summer of 1818, Percy Shelley stayed in this Spa town with his wife Mary, and Claire Claremont - the girlfriend he shared with Gordon Byron. They rented a small villa, the Casa Bertini, overlooking the oldest of the marble spas, lying next to the disused chapel of the Grand Duke of Tuscany. They were surrounded by chestnut woods, which rose steeply to the mountain peaks on both sides of the Lima River - tumbling far below with rampant impetuousness towards the Serchio River and the sea.

The Grand Duke was holding court. Bagni di Lucca was the glittering epicentre of the Season, which had started at the end of June. The place was overwhelmed by smart *Inglese*, *Stranieri* and *Dilettante*. They hoped to bump into the flavour of the month - Princess Pauline Buonaparte, who was Napoleon's sister, and married to Prince Camilo Borghese. She had taken the title of Empress of Tuscany. The English hangers-on and social climbers grovelled all over her, conveniently forgetting they had just captured and exiled her brother. Balls, soirees, dances, masquerades, and river parties were in full swing, mainly in the villas which sprawl along both sides of the Lima River. The carriages of the nobles knocked the carts of the locals, as they wended their way in a wild spree along the rough riverside track which joined the three hamlets of this bubbling little town. It was summer; and only in summer did the Lima Valley come to life. It was *the* place to be. In the town square and private gardens, the game of *Palla a Maglio* (Ball to Mallet) was earnestly played. This was a cross between bowls and croquet, and its popularity had reached such a craze in England that *Palla a Maglio* had given its name to Pall Mall - the swanky London street in the heart of club-land, where Italian style Palazzi were being built for Regency bucks.

Taking the waters of the sulphur and calcium springs from several spas, Percy and Mary hung out in the quiet atmosphere of Bagni di Lucca's heavenly extremity. They avoided the torrid English 'trippers' and paparazzi who came to ogle Princess Pauline.

Their small villa, the Casa Bertini, hidden high up in the chestnut woods, was reached on foot up a narrow cobbled mule track, or on horseback from the excellent stables down in the town. They were well away from the dank, dark and dangerous river valley where it never stops raining for long in winter; and even in summer can feel like England on a bad day.

The wild woods brought out the primal urge in Percy to scream, howl and dance: "My custom is to undress and sit on the rocks, read Heroditus until the perspiration has subsided, and then to leap from the rock into the fountain".

He clamoured to escape his northern European inhibitions, and rode a few kilometres up to the *Prato Fiorito* - the flowering meadow, high in the Apennines where the Golden Eagle still roams above the wooded hills that reach up to the peaks. Mary reluctantly followed suit. She later declared: "We lived in utter solitude".

Naturally oversensitive, Percy was overwhelmed by vivid violets, white jonquils, and scarlet peonies which caused him to fall into a cataclysm of almost orgasmic complexity. He was one of the first to experience the onset of the one 'disease' which is still taken seriously in Tuscany. It mainly affects tired and overawed Culture Vultures. Gordon Byron and the art critic John Ruskin, also fell for it. 'Stendahl's Syndrome', also known as the Santa Croce effect, had just been discovered by the French novelist and diplomat Stendahl in 1817. It is caused by the intake of too many beautiful things. He first recorded the head spinning, mind-boggling disorientation, when he nearly fell over backwards looking up at Giotto's earthy frescoes on the ceiling of Santa Croce in Florence. "Life was drained from me", he recalled, "I walked with fear of falling over". Italian doctors still admit that this 'sickness' can cause dizziness, panic, the shakes, paranoia and even madness. It is mainly evident in Florence. The cure is simple; avoid Tuscany and its beauty like the plague. Cast a beady eye on all things awful and repulsive, and turn your minds eye to other thoughts.

**Between the thud of falling chestnuts
and the groaning of the stream -
sounds which join together -
the heart hesitates**.

Bagni di Lucca - Eugenio Montale

We were crossing the main square in Bagni di Lucca. Nearby a rather ordinary looking house, now turned into a small block of flats, boasted another blue plaque of Shelley's short sojourn. Once more, the inscription recorded his brooding on free love and revolution.

Just around the corner we wandered into the square dominated by the *Circolo dei Forestiere* - the Circle for Foreigners - once the meeting place for the *Glitterati* and *Literati*. And here the whole nineteenth century Tuscan saga unfolded before our eyes. The front of the building had been draped in the old colours of the Grand Old Duchy of Tuscany. Modern street lamps had been converted to shady old braziers. An elegant carriage rattled across the square, pulled by two lithe black nags. Seated inside this elegant quadriga was a lady with a parasol, accompanied by her swain - dressed like Beau Brummell. The open square was dotted with vegetable sellers standing at stalls. Women were carrying fruit baskets and flagons of wine. A local urchin made a V sign at a man in uniform. The Postilion jumped down from the carriage as it pulled up in front of the building, emblazoned with bunting. The young lady jumped out, and rushed across the square into the arms of her lover.

The 1800's spring to life. Then all of a sudden: '*Movimento*!" cries the film director. "Action!" It started to rain like cats and dogs. I turn to see a group of Italians directing hoses at flat roofs which bounce water off the walls and drench the proceedings. As the horses stand shivering, the whole square erupts. "Cut!" shouts the film director, as the camera rolls forward and slithers to a skidding halt. He shouts at the men with the hoses, whose timing has been less than perfect, to direct their attention elsewhere. The camera rolls back on its tracks and the scene is retaken, again and again.

The Film, which rather takes the piss out of the eternal triangle of international events, is an elaborate 1800's romantic costume drama.

The film crew adjourned to the café on the corner of the Square. I propped myself against the bar, whilst the girls grabbed a table. The young English Actor was in full-on soliloquy mode: "I am not really the lead actor. There isn't much dialogue, anyway. It's mostly dubbed afterwards. We only mouth our words; to match with the lip synchronisation later.

"It is the story of Emily, a delicate young lady who is prone to fainting fits. Her husband, a famous archaeologist, has just died. I play the role of his English assistant and I accompany her back to Italy, where we are digging up the ruins of an ancient temple. She agrees to marry me, although I'm not exactly the world's greatest Casanova. True to form, Emily meets a dashing Italian Army Doctor, just returned from the colonies, and falls for him. We are all staying at the nearby hotel here, in this famous spa town. The local innkeeper warns her that he is a notorious ladies man, but she ditches me, and runs off with him. That's the gist of the story."

It's the eternal triangle that could have been taken from any age, when many of the notorious ladies of the day were vulnerable to the predators of the times.

For Bagni di Lucca was on the 'Grand Tour of Decadence'. To avoid the worst weather and the most boring society, every well-to-do traveller swaggered in here, on their perambulations around Tuscany. It also became the mecca for English, French and German writers and poets.

The English Cemetery is all that is left, with a few pious plaques in the old Anglican Church – now the Library.

One of the most majestic of all figures to pass through this tiny spa town was almost unknown. Henry, Cardinal Duke of York was the younger brother of Bonnie Prince Charlie.

Their father, the Old Pretender, had visited Bagni di Lucca in the 1770's. In a fit of jealous revenge, King George III of England threatened an embargo on Lucca's famous Olive Oil. His eldest son was the Young Pretender, Charles Edward Stuart, who was both Pretender to the English Throne, and the last real King of Scotland. He claimed the title Charles III, after his courageous army had been annihilated at the massacre of Culloden near Inverness. That Battle largely destroyed the passionate cohesion of the clan system. He escaped firstly to France, and then went to live in exile in Rome. After his death in drunken middle age, his younger brother Henry, Duke of York, who was born and brought up in Rome, then claimed the title of heir presumptive to the English throne. So the little known Henry became the very last of the Stuart clan who laid claim to the thrones of both England and Scotland. When he came to the Baths of Lucca, he was already an ordained priest and a Cardinal. He arrived in a carriage, amid much fanfare. Unlike many of the scheming Cardinals of the day, he was admired, respected and successful, being one of the Roman Curia's favourites. So it was quite likely that as Henry, Cardinal Duke of York he could well have become both King of England and Pope at the same time. Thus, he could have restored both the old Monarchy, and the old Faith, to England's green and pleasant land.

The Browning's spent quieter times here. Robert Browning brought his ailing sister Elizabeth, and both poets found romance and health in the spa town. He made her sip the local Tuscan wine to wean her off her addiction to Opium, known in polite society as Laudanum. She had been hooked on it since a teenager, to cure her of the middle class Victorian disease of *Narcissistic Hypochondria*, brought on when it was smart to be 'pale and interesting'. They spent most of their time avoiding the locals, and like the Shelley's, 'lived in utter solitude'. In the true spirit of the age they became morbidly romantic, whilst reading the best poets of the day - namely Byron, Shelley, Keats and Wordsworth.

**"Open my heart and you will see**
**Grained inside of it – 'Italy'!"**
*Robert Browning:  De Gustibus 1855.

Just up from Bagni Di Lucca, in the mountains towards the ski resort of Abetone, can be seen both the

Seas of Italy – the Tyrrhenian on one side, and the Adriatic on the other. Here, where Golden Eagles prowl, the very rare Apennine species of wolves howl in the misty hills. From the highest points you can even see as far as the French Alps, and Monte Cinto on the island of Corsica. The composer Puccini had a house here, to escape the hottest summer months in the plains below.

Back on track from Bagni di Lucca Station we hurry, halt and judder on our way up the valley. Here and there, along the river banks, we spy huge modern storage sheds, stacked outside with giant room-sized cubes - perhaps 10 cubic metres. They are huge parcels of discarded paper, ready for shredding, pulping and recycling in these mundane riverside plants where millions of gallons of water are used. From a distance, in size, shape and colour, they mirror exactly the huge marble blocks which lie on the other, seaward side of the mountain - only 20 kilometres as the crow flies across to the quarries of Carrara.

The Garfagnana lies ahead. It is neither the name of a local cheese; nor a variety of mushroom or truffle. GAR-FAG-NA-NA – (the first vowel repeated 4 times over), is the district of mountains, glens, valleys, and dales between the Apennines and the Apuan Alps which border the sea.

Onwards and upwards, we clackety-clack round a corner with a resounding screech. We shudder over a level crossing of pole barriers. As the scraping wheels shrill against the curve, a mechanical cowbell melodically warns the road traffic of our approach.

Suddenly we are launched into an open vista of winding lanes that run up into the hills, towards villages perched abruptly on both sides of the Serchio River Valley. God's glories lie above; human howlers lie below.

All of a sudden, industrial Italy has been left behind. Mercifully.

This land of Wolves and Outlaws has more than a touch of Scotland about it. It is real Haggis and Trout country. Lush pastures and bracing streams. Walter Scott territory. The author of so many lusty ballads and melodramas of the Highlands; of Mediaeval Castles and fierce Clans in fiery fiefdoms, of misty lakes with submerged villages, and lonesome lovers, was almost lifted from here. Inevitably, Rob Roy's and Ivanhoe's descendants still lurk around the rustic corners.

In the early 1800's, Walter Scott pandered to the public's thirst for romance and adventure, He combined a love for the past with a sense of the modern. He held the reins of poetic power over his half Scottish friend Gordon Byron, eighteen years his junior. Byron denigrated Scott. Meanwhile Scott's friend Robert Southey, who had been handed the 'Poet Laureateship' on a plate by Scott, attacked both Byron and Shelley in print for their bad poetry and worse morals. *(Southey's wife went mad, and his sister-in-law hanged herself)*.

Yet both these literary lions, Scott and Byron, with gammy legs, would have been at ease in these foothills of the Apennines. They would have hobbled along gamely on sticks, stomping around these passionate landscapes, tapping away at the stony ruins, and rapping away with a hidden fiery admiration for each other.

"From a boy I always did like an argument", Byron admitted to Scott. He was envious of his rival's nonchalance, unpretentious attitude, and his unliterary approach to life.

As a 'defeated' publisher, Scott had switched his remarkable talents from Poetry to romantic Tales, to earn enough money to pay off the huge debts of the bankrupt Ballantyne's Publishers, in which he was a partner with his friend John Ballantyne. He bore this humiliation with great fortitude and dignity. It was a remarkably courageous act which eclipsed his life, sending him to an early grave. He literally wrote himself to death. Hospitable, hard working and hard drinking, he would have been inspired by this land of warring cities and clashing clans calling from the glens. His story of feuding in The Lady of the Lake was all about a mysterious, itinerant Knight. Two years later Gordon Byron followed the tale with his own metaphorical Childe Harold's Pilgrimage. This was his autobiographical account of wandering through a similar world – this time in Italy.

In a parallel way, Gordon Byron also redeemed his family's misfortunes. Within days of publication of his eagerly awaited poems, tens of thousands of copies were sold, enabling him to continue his *louche* lifestyle. He was further motivated because his profligate uncle had sold off most of his inheritance, and his mad Scottish mother - a Gordon – had lost her lands.

Byron and Scott also shared the same enigmatic figures of heraldry. Their Coats of Arms were emblazoned with Mermaids. By tradition, sightings of mermaids were said to herald bad omens, foretelling treacherous storms, rough seas and death on the waves.

The forests and glens of Garfagnana are reminiscent of northern climes. Even the soil has that saturated boggy peat look about it. Pine and Chestnuts add to the character of it. Misty, drizzling rain, driven by the mountains, is the very essence of the climate which Byron endured in Aberdeen for 9 years. It drove him, like so many other restless and spirited Scotsmen, with a few plucky Scots lasses, out into a world from where they could satisfy their craving for space, silence and sunshine. The world in which they were able to pioneer for Great Britain, an Empire as great and powerful as the Roman one.

There is still an unofficial gathering of clans here. They are the Scots-Italians, descendants of those who emigrated over the last century to Caledonia, made their fortune in Ice Cream and Fish & Chips, and then returned to their former roots.

"Ecco Lo. There he is. The dead man!" exclaimed Angela as we rattled onwards towards Barga.

Across the highest peaks of the Apuan Alps facing the sea, an old man lies sound asleep. He is embarked on an eternal watch, to prevent a young lady from crossing over the mountains from the coast to the Garfagnana region, in her quest to join up with an unsuitable lover. He will only wake up if she dares to trespass across his dizzy threshold.

So goes the legend of the *Uomo Morto of Monte Forato*, in the shape of a prone man lying along the ridge of mountains on the seaward side of the Apuan Alps. These are Italy's unknown Alps wedged between the Ligurian Sea and the Apennines with peaks that reach 1800 metres high, at a distance less than 8 miles from the coast, as the gulls fly. Dozens of dizzy villages cling to high mountain-sides. Long abandoned forts and five hundred year old monasteries, bolted to bedrock, still dominate the passes through the valleys, which gurgle with rivers full of trout. Alongside, Italy's cave system extends through gorges of stalactites and stalagmites.

It was here that the canny Irishman Saint Frediano came back to meditate. And once again he confronted the devil on his way over from the ocean. He hurled the demon with such force that it was sent crashing through the mountain back into the sea, knocking a hole in the peak of Monte Forato - which today forms the open mouth of the *Uomo Morto*.

When the torrential rains hit these high mountains; they become rolling lands where nothing will stop growing. Or stand still. All hell breaks loose in one of the wettest areas of Italy. Even villages have been swept away.

The clouds roll in from the Tyrrhenian Sea, thundering over the Apuan Alps. The hot air from the valleys rises in turmoil, and brings down thunder and lightning. Wave after wave of cascading water is driven horizontally by the air currents. Only the highest mountains are immune. The snow capped Apennines are left untouched. Far below the snowline, every living creature cowers into submission, hiding in nooks and crannies to escape the downpour.

The villages below the *Uomo Morto* bear the full brunt. Vineyards, sharply built on terraces up the mountainside, are ripped to their roots. Silently the storm steals a march. At that stage the only sound is from inside the buildings, as the gathering tempest thunders down on the terracotta tiles, stealing relentlessly through the tiny gaps and fissures that allow the roof to breathe. The solid stone houses take a lashing; but appear impermeable. As the deluge continues, only large gullies and gutters can handle it. Fast flowing rivulets become raging torrents, as the downpour swirls down the narrow streets, engulfing the drains, clogged with debris. Roaring over the open grids, unable to cope, the Surge spills out between the houses. Gravity drags it onwards. Cracks appear in stone walls. On every square metre of ground half a ton of water falls in 14 hours. The force beats on, tearing away at the foundations, and all of a sudden the wall gives way, riven to its roots. The massive stone structure expunges through the gap. The Torrent rips over the next terrace, roars on, and hits the foundations of the houses below. With a crash, the outbuilding collapse. Hen-runs and chicken-dens disappear in the tidal flow. The birds fly up in terror to escape the onslaught, drenched and drowned.

Now a sea of mud appears, mixed with the debris of rocks and stones, and remains of concrete foundations. This abrasive march thunders on further, destroying everything in its path. The final massive wall supporting the road collapses down the valley. Half the village of Cardoso slides down the mountainside. The Divine Comedy becomes Dante's Inferno.

**Listen, listen Mary mine,**
**to the whisper of the Apennine.**
**It bursts on the roof like the thunders roar;**
**Or like the sea on a northern shore.** [3]

Far below, the railway continues along the river bank of the Serchio, past villages perched upon either side. Past *Coreglia Antelminelli* – 'Liza Minelli' in Brit speak, from where many emigrants were driven to the Big Apple. Their unique and legendary skills as figurine makers went with them.

The line runs into the centre of the local powerhouse - *Fornaci di Barga*. The Furnace of Barga.

Before WW1, there was clamour on all sides to bring the railway up from Lucca to the 'promised land of opportunity'. The only alternative was to emigrate to America. Many did, and every spring and summer the lucky ones who had made it in the Big Apple came back by sea to visit their relatives. They sported all the flashy trappings of the New World - watches and gold rings, new clothes and the latest fashions.

The prospect of the railway bringing work to all sides of the valley forged the hopes and dreams of the young who were left behind.

In the summer of 1912 the rail service between Lucca and Castelnuovo was finally opened, with trains running four times a day. So the Furnace of Barga was on the map, wallowing in new prosperity.

There was silver and manganese ore, deposits of asbestos and lignite, as well as timber and agricultural produce from the surrounding valleys. Riches of all kinds were railed down to the coast. Along the line of rail itself, people flocked to set up strategically placed local businesses such as charcoal burning, and Fruit & Vegetable Markets.

World War I brought a halt to the flood of Italians who travelled back from America. Whilst Britain and America controlled the Oceans with a naval blockade, crossing the Atlantic was a dodgy business. Italy joined in the hostilities, and *Fornaci di Barga* was finally transformed from a backward agricultural community into a real blazing furnace for armaments and ammunition.

Today it makes aperitifs and liqueurs, as well as delicate metal inlays for the two-toned coins of the new Realm of Europe.

[1]  Shelley: Lines written among the Euganean Hills 1818
[2]  Shelley: The Boat on the Serchio 1821
[3]   Shelley: Passage to the Apennines

# Chapter 4

# BARGA

~~~~

As the train rumbled into Barga Galicano, a statue of Padre Pio greeted me reverently from the Station car park. Trust in him - I thought. For this is earthquake territory, where house insurance is a nightmare.

The Padre continued to stare back at me as I waited for two hours to catch a bus up to Barga. I lost faith in buses.

So I walked up the hill from the Station. In my mind's eye I was sweating at the distance on the map. It was a twisty road, about three kilometres long, that wormed its way upwards through the woods, zig-zagging backwards and forwards as it climbed. Sometimes a bus, going elsewhere, switch-backed down the narrow road, greeting every corner with its two-toned melody. So, I took the short direct route, walking straight through the woods to avoid the bends.

And then, on almost the last twist of all – in a clearing of trees, I stopped to look at the sweeping view across the valley. I turned to hear the sound of tumbling water. It ran from a hidden brook, out of the hillside, gurgling and bubbling into an ancient stone cattle trough, deep enough to take a bath in. I took off my shirt, and drenched my face and arms in the ice cold torrent. A neat little sign exclaimed: *Acqua non potabile*. In gorgeous English, someone had added: Not to Drink! This is crazy. Pure water from out of the Apennines! I cupped my hands with glee and took a long draught. It was sweet and unsullied. I rolled up my trousers, and hung my aching feet over the edge of the stone trough. The sun glared down, prancing through the branches of the trees. A few birds swooped, and I sensed the blissful rustle of rural Tuscany.

I lay down on some leaves in a grassy spot among boulders, and dozed off, thinking of the wine and *prosciutto* I should have brought with me. The rustling stopped, as the lizards and animals crept away for their own siesta. I was left alone.

There was nothing to hear except *a little noiseless noise among the leaves, born of the very sigh that silence heaves.*[1]
The insects woke early. I was buzzed and bombarded with a vengeance, and stirred to the sound of church bells ringing the Angelus.

Barga was nearer than I expected. There on the hill-crest perched the tiny sunlit town - shimmering like a New Jerusalem. The citadel was surrounded on all sides by elegant, rampant walls which had repelled countless invaders. They came up the valleys from the rich cities of the Tuscan plains, to lay claim to this industrious little mountain stronghold. The hard working locals had no chance. In those moments of high dudgeon, it was a sort of reverse Robin Hood effect - stealing from the poor to give to the rich.

For me, it was a 'green light' up to the *Fosso* –

the irreverently named Ditch, where a moat once ran round the city walls. Alongside the *Porta Reale* – the Royal Gate of King Victor Emmanuel, the ancient symbol of the city once stood. It was a majestic Cedar of Lebanon tree, overlooking a huge open terrace. It was planted in 1823, only a few months after Percy Shelley was drowned on the coast below, and a year before the death of Gordon Byron in Greece. In that same year, the poet William Blake penned his verse to 'those dark satanic hills in England's green and pleasant land'. Two years later, in 1825, Britain entered the industrial revolution with George Stephenson's launch of the world's first railway journey between Stockton and Darlington.

For nearly two centuries, this remarkable Cedar had stood the test of time. Like a giant parasol, it overshadowed the main entrance into Barga, where the old folk clustered around the car-park, chattering and nattering, and refreshing themselves in many of the best taverns in town.

> *The righteous shall grow like a palm tree, and flourish like a Cedar of Lebanon.*

The Bible was right. Wide and flourishing the tree once was. Then it was no more. Sadly, the poisoned earth took its toll. A hardy new sapling was nourished in the ground where the old cedar once stood.

As I ventured into the city under a time-warped mediaeval portcullis, I felt I was trespassing. It was as if time had stood still, and the builders had taken another day off. I gazed up in search of some meaningful majestic icon of renaissance significance. I searched in vain. All I saw were the battered stone Coats of Arms of the local hierarchy who once prospered here. I felt a little lonely and depressed. It was a sombre reversal of the Santa Croce Effect. I wandered through the narrow cobbled streets, past dark and formidable alleyways with steep stone staircases that went onwards and upwards. The *Vicolo del Sole* - Sunshine Alley - stood with no sunshine at all. Then I suddenly turned into a cosy little square with window boxes, and gazed into more formidable passageways - hung not with washing, but with real geraniums, in shimmering sunlight.

*'Se ha ragione, non ha paura'.*

'If you are right, fear not', repeated another truly Tuscan saying on the walls of an advocates house.

All 'roads' climbed up to the ancient Cathedral. Inside, a 700 year old marble font greeted me.. It looked mightily tempting - guarded by two benevolent marble lions. One of them was crushing a serpent, and the other eating – presumably - a Luccan or a Pisan. On high days and holidays, the challenge of the local children was – traditionally - to ride these sturdy creatures, and beat the living daylights out of them.

Once it was the barrow boys and muleteers who sweated their way up those narrow alleyways to bring in the provisions. Nowadays, Barga's streets are just wide enough to squeeze through a Ka or the odd Topolino – the famous old mickey-mouse baby Fiat And the cobblestones are still patronised by alley cats. Some are well fed, plump and prosperous looking. Others are sleek, white and aristocratic looking.

When the Medici's invented banking in Florence, and expanded into all sorts of other trades, Barga spawned a bank of its own. If quantity is a symbol of bureaucracy, or pious prosperity, then prosperous old Barga had 7 churches - as well as 7 banks, and the Post Office.

Most moved down to the new town.

Yet the Seat of Power, the Town Hall, is still where it all started - next to the Café Capretz. In its cool corners, the smartest wheeling and dealing once took place. And sometimes still does. From the balcony of this ancient aristocratic coffee house, one could spy ones enemies sidling up the walkway through one of the city's three gateways.

From this same balcony, in the early 1900's, the great 'Poet of the People', Giovanni Pascoli, word-smithed his way into modern Italian minds. Musing with melancholy over flagons of wine, he gazed for inspiration across the Serchio valley, where he lived with his sister in rural harmony.

**'Here lies Beauty and Goodness, and it is here that I would like to remain'**, he wrote.

(Qui c'e  Belo̊, e c'e Buonò ed e qui che vogliò restare.)

Nothing could be more sublime.

His poetry combined the sights, sounds and scents of the local landscapes and sky-scopes. The mountains, trees, animals, crops, food and the 'simple life' were woven into the everyday language of the people. Like the Odes of John Keats, it was toe-curling poetry with the common touch.

**Into my quiet corner, where my ears strain**
**to the chaffing of the grain,**
**the Sound of the Hour is carried on the wind**
**from an unseen mountain tower.**
**It's an even sound, that blandly cascades,**
**like a voice that gently persuades.** [2]

> Al mio cantuccio, donde non sento
> Se non le reste brusir del grano,
> Il suon dell'ore viene col vento
> Dal non veduto borgo montano;
> suono che uguale, che blando cade,
> come una voce che persuade.

From the *Arringo* surrounding the Cathedral, Pascoli *harangued* the masses before World War I. The takeover of Tripoli and North Africa from the Turks was the flavour of the month.

His upbringing encouraged more than a sense of poetic justice. Many of his poems were inspired by family tragedies. The assassination of his father, and the early deaths of his mother and five of his brothers & sisters, nurtured deep emotions. He responded to this loss by becoming a fiery radical at Bologna University. Like Shelley before him, his anarchist views landed him in trouble. He went to prison.

Barga's bells tolled the curfew at 9 o'clock in winter and 10 o'clock in summer, when the great wooden gates were locked and barred from strangers.

I walked unhindered through the same empty

gateways whose stone hinges were still intact. I pondered the same clangs, as I realised that we were still required to rest our limbs in this little corner of Tuscany, and rise at the crack of dawn to enjoy the fruits of our labours.

Like many self-sustaining Italian towns, still remote from modern rat-race, the crime rate remained low. Everyone knew everyone. Strangers stood out like sore thumbs. Behind shuttered windows, the ladies of the house kept watch from the battlements. The doors and shutters banged shut against dark strangers hocking socks and sunglasses.

In this *Piccolo Paradiso* there was little need of the *Polizia*. People looked after their own, and children were brought up in the spirit of self denial, when Barga was a cut above the average. For what was Italy? Only a conglomeration of feuding clans and independent minds, where the Family comes first, the Province second and the Country third.

Spontaneous music erupted from around the corner. I turned into a square in the corner of that timeless mediaeval central 'patch', which every Tuscan City worth its salt can boast. As always, the commercial hub is where the flotsam and jetsam meet and greet, along with the Great and the Good. I passed by a faded sign of a once thriving *Spaghetteria,* looking like it was doomed since Mussolini's time. A shop next door boasted various local products "As sold to Mussolini on his visit here" recited a cardboard sign advertising Cheese. In the next Piazza was a fabulous faded remnant of a *Macelleria*, closed long ago. Around the corner, outside an antique shop, the forlorn owner was selling antiques 'on consignment' - a polite Italian term for sale or return.

As the rich American said: "I never saw a quainter corner." There I found a sign saying simply: *Ferreteria* - Ironmongery. I wandered in, thinking of scintillating chrome fixtures, shiny electric irons and coffee machines with cappuccino spouts. Modern Italian design. Instead, in the dim cavern, I discerned - hanging grimly from the walls and ceilings - brackets and chains, cast iron grids, and grills for open stoves, alongside mediaeval pots, metal pinchers and grappling hooks; as well as hatchets, ratchets and adzes that looked like the Chamber of Horrors. These tools had curiously stood the test of time. Yet I couldn't imagine when they were used. Or even what they were for. The moustachioed Luca was serving a customer – evidently one of the many Scots in these parts.

"*Dica* !" he demands.

"Masonry nails?" He demonstrated with his finger stuck in a hole in the wall. Luca shuffled through a battery of little drawers in an ancient chestnut cabinet, one at a time, searching relentlessly. He scrabbled around to find what look like little pieces of hand hammered metal.

"A Hammer?" The distracted customer looked up earnestly at rows of axes, saws, pokers, and weapons of mass destruction, trying hard to locate one.

"*Forza!*" He demonstrated in best Italian, thumping his fists together, then down on the wooden counter. Luca went to the back of the shop and then calmly returned with a rusty metal hammer-head. It looked like a mini executioners axe. He produced a wooden handle, and assembled the weapon painlessly. With a deft whack of the wrist, he cleft a metal wedge into the top end of the wooden handle, which secured the hammer-head tightly. Miraculously, another antique weapon was conjured up.

*"Forza!"* he reiterated.

*"Gomma per la finestra?"* the Scotsman asked. (Putty for the window?). The real Macoy arrived - not out of a modern silicone tube. A wedge of disgustingly oily putty was sliced with a knife, and slapped onto a sheet of torn newspaper. It was weighed on the scale, and wrapped like a piece of Mozzarella cheese. It was then wacked onto the wooden counter - just like the butcher's block down the road.

*"Nient Altro?"* he enquired. The man handed him a £5 note. Bank of Scotland version. Then he beamed.

*"Mia moglie e Scozzeze"*, he declared, *"Sempre vuole trovare questi"*. (My wife is Scottish - always looking for these). He kissed it religiously.

*"Grazie Grazie. Keep the change."*

Outside the shop next door, I was greeted by an array of smiling faces painted on colourful umbrellas hanging below the balcony.

There were benches against the wall, with rustic tables and wobbly stools. From behind a beaded plastic curtain, spontaneous music erupted, punctuated by raucous laughter. I wandered in, thinking nostalgically of a cross between a jazz joint and an old time music hall. Like many strangers, I had stumbled upon *Aristodemo's* - perhaps the most memorable and least known, but best loved 'local' in that extremity of Tuscany. It was the Osteria Casciani, then known more endearingly as 'Aristo's', run by the sprightly Arostodemo Casciani and his family. It was once an *Alimentari,* a groovy Grocery shop which evolved into a spontaneous rustic Wine Bar of remarkable simplicity, durability and notoriety. It also sold bread, ham, cheese and the necessities. Rolling around in the wine, for 50 cents a glass, were most of the regulars. Who could deny them this simple joy - with the chance of some of the best local cheeses? A few bottles of wine stood on the shelves, but mostly it was sold by the flagon or tumbler-full. Not everyone's cup of tea, perhaps a little too jovial, but it was proof that the simple personality business reigned supreme.

Hams and Salamis hung from the ceiling. The atmosphere was interrupted by the sound of a modern machine, slicing paper-thin *Prosciutto.* On the shelves stood a formidable collection of over 300 bottles, which had accumulated since the *Alimentari* flourished before the last War. Most were from long forgotten local companies, such as the enterprising monks of Lucca who produced liqueurs and spirits of mesmerising variety and complexity.

"Every single bottle is a relic; a little piece of our history. They are beautiful, timeless pictures – like Tintoretto or Botticelli", declared Aristodemo. He kissed the sexy image on the label of a Grappa Nardini.

"Indestructible! They all have a value to my family. This is the 1938 Anisetta of my grandmother" he proudly expounded, with a twinkle in his eye and an amber look of self assurance. There stood a bottle of a rare Acquavita, which was a wedding present to him and his wife. Alongside was a bottle of Tre Valetti, with its label of three valets carrying a massive flagon on their shoulders.

Aristodemo and Barga were both on the 'Grand Tour'. Not the one of the Romantic Poets, or the Ladies with smelling salts. This was the modern 1980's version of Russell Harty for BBC Television. They pitched up with a camera crew, and made a big song and dance, whilst interviewing the star player Aristo. Harty couldn't understand a word of Italian. There was a smattering of English from Aristo. It was pronounced so enchantingly, that he stood his ground firmly, whilst the cameras rolled on. He was trying to describe the 'Speciality of the House'. "Cheeeps Seeeze." he kept repeating. You mean Cheap Cheese? Chips Please? No! After several takes, it turned out to be "Sheep's Cheese." It was the perfect recipe for good goggling.

*Tutto riesce con calma!* - All succeeds with calmness.

Aristo spent his whole life in Barga. "For over 60 years I walked back and forth to the Osteria, and every time it seemed like I came back here for the first time. This is a record of my life since 1938. I was eight when Mussolini came to Barga in 1932." Il Duce enjoyed the panorama so much that he never went outside Barga. He inferred a city status on it. "All these immortal liquors," he explains as he shrugs, "have survived a World War, and have followed all the ups and downs of my life. It's in my blood - also my two predecessors - my grandfather Aristodemo, and my father Felice."

Now the custodians of this happy world are his daughters and son-in-law.

"They are following in my footsteps" he assured me.

Alongside a picture of the Madonna and Child, a portrait of his father once hung in pride of place. Photographs were propped in various corners. Certificates presented by the local Commune were in grateful recognition of his *buon compagno ai stranieri* - his hospitality to strangers, and his celebration of Christmas in the 'customary way'. Tradition stood proud here. It was as a sort of Club, where you could pick up the local gossip. It's where the Contadini met the Cittadini, or where the Rusticati met the Urbani – the Simple folk meet the Spoilt folk. For Aristo's Bar still stands bang opposite the Palazzo Pretorio - the ancient symbol of aristocratic privilege. Salute !

In time worn tradition, Aristo proceeded with ageless dexterity to siphon off some wine from a gigantic glass flagon, covered in raffia, which was perched on a wobbly stool. He sucked on a plastic tube, drew breath, and with perfect timing, the wine was released by gravity into the litre flasks - ready for instant take-away, or instant quaffing. He poured me a neat splurge into a mini tumbler and winked: "Very good! - from Montecarlo", he declared. It was a light red wine from the town of that name in the hills above Lucca. Like many of the best Tuscan Wines, it was almost unknown outside the area. The Wine of Montecarlo, known as *Lo Chablis di Montecarlo*, was once served at the wedding of the last King of Italy.

His daughter was at the bar; his son-in-law was

busy at the back, slicing the paper thin ham. I helped myself to a sample of mountain *prosciutto* as near to the Parma variety as possible. Without the price tag. I was then introduced to the flavour of the month – a mountain goat cheese - with another nod and a wink. Aristo did it in a way that only the Italians can do, adding a few words of mesmerising complexity - not words of sense, but of great sensitivity. You guess and you greet. And when you analyse it, absolutely nothing has been said at all.

The locals appeared. One by one, they trotted in, and stomped out. *'Sempre ciucco, mai malato',* (Always smashed, never ill): quipped Boccacio – the one with the big mouth. The Angel and the Witch passed by. The party started. Was that the man I was looking for? Piombino, the local plumber, sat in the corner with the miraculous Marcella, whose knowledge of men from 18 to 80 was prodigious. A touch scruffy, she arrived as if she had just been dragged out of the Serchio River. Propped against the bar was Alberto, the florid, jovial professor from the north of England. His family emigrated during the recession. He returned to his roots. A young English lass popped in. She bought her house down the road from an Italian 'acquaintance', who won it over a game of cards with his neighbour, after they couldn't agree who owned it.

There harped Papagino from the Magic Flute, with eyes like an eagle, and a nose like a hawk. He sniffed out the local *funghi porchini*, and brought them into town as fast as lightning. From his devilish basket he dragged out some Satanoides, and some erotic looking Phalloides. In all shapes and sizes. Most mesmerising of all were mushrooms that looked like a bunch of brains. He carried his card from the Mayor, the *permesso* that allowed him to wander the woods and lanes of the Garfagnana in search of nature's trophies. Others were jealous.

*Then one warm night, when the sun fell down behind the Dead Man's mountain, this gentle Man of the Woods flew away to Heaven, on the soft summer wind, from the edge of the Ponte. And everyone missed him.*

At the bar stood an aristocratic looking Italian who resembled Gordon Byron. He was a communist advocate with an aquiline nose, a sardonic smile, and the dignity of a Renaissance courtier. It was the same classic Etruscan profile that I observed down at Pisa.

He launched into historic name-dropping.

"We are all Etruscans from where I come from - down the coast. We are not Romans! We beat the Romans. We beat them in art, literature and style of living. Our women were even superior. We Etruscans invented pasta long before the Romans arrived, and centuries before Marco Polo brought some back from China. Our language is the purest in Italy. It became the accent for the whole country. Dante Aligheri from Florence saw to that".

The Professor chirped in: "Some say: *Lingua Toscana in Bocca Romana*" – the Tuscan tongue sounds best in a Roman mouth.

There sat Godfrey, the Italian-American, a descendant of one of those who left to prosper in the powerhouse of Industry. He offered to sell me his car. "I am going back to die in Chicago," he declared in a perfect mid-west accent. "This place hasn't changed since I left 50 years ago. It bores me." I commented: How do you translate. "Do you know the one about the beautiful lady who meets the Italian in the bar?" He didn't wait for my reply.

A stranded exile dropped in from the coast, along with a dress designer from Chelsea, to join two rich Americans. A marketing man from London, who worked through the Internet, celebrated at the bar. A wonderful woman I spied, in floral dress, was redolent of Chris de Burgh's Irish heroine. She only entered for *desperado Vino*, quaffed one, and disappeared. This was not a woman's world. Except on music nights, which were spontaneous.

Music was in Aristo's blood. In perfect harmony, deft fingers that have just drawn the wine from the flagon turned to a light, leisurely flourish across the keyboard of an electric organ piano. He struck up an Italianised rendition of *'Spanish Eyes'*. This performance was punctuated by various asides to nearby patrons and accompanying banjo, mandolin and guitar players.

There fiddled the Salesman who worked the World, and dived back to Barga for breakfast with his wife. A hardy *Geometra* strummed a guitar. The multi talented journalist was as keen as a whistle. The laid-back customers watched like weasels, and hummed like tossers. One of the three witches wandered by. A lovely local lass led the chorus.

Aristo was multi-lingual; and sometimes monosyllabic. He drew the rapturous audience into the rhythm. All were seduced by the atmosphere. He was no mean Bottle Player. The maestro demonstrated his expertise. He grabbed a couple of long metal desert spoons, and standing behind the counter, proceeded to ring the tones up and down the bottles ranged along the shelf. He harmonised his light voice with the timbres on the prearranged glassware. Those in the middle had deep tones, those at the end were of a lighter key. Bottles of Gancia and Vecchia Romana had a note of B Sharp and E flat about them. The almost empty bottle of Rammazottit had a *tremolando* that sounded slightly off key - and looked off colour.

As Arisoto pranced up and down, playing the scales and singing wildly, the rhythm increased. This feisty gig continued with a kick like a chorus line. His vocal accompaniment gained new heights. '*La Paloma*' had never been rendered with such gusto and agility. All in perfect harmony, the strident tones of this 'Fantasia on Bottles' reached a crescendo - with a resounding crash on the Gambarotta. The bottle cracked. It was a very rare vintage. Aristo beamed with toothless delight.

As I looked up at the last bottle of Grappa Julia, I pondered. Even if we could not understand one another - neither the mad songs nor my faltering accent - there was music and wine between us all; and the local cheese and ham, and bread - which is the bond of all mankind. Happy days!

I walked – as did everyone else on the *Passegiata* through the empty streets – to restore my faith in human nature.

Down the alleyway, a marble memorial on the wall recorded the referendum of 1946, in which 12.7

million Italians voted for the abolition of their Monarchy. 10.7 million voted to retain it. It was a tight margin for the Republicans.

Over a united Italy the monarchy lasted only eighty years. It began with an episode in the 1860's, which boasted graffiti with hidden meaning. The letters V.E.R.D.I. appeared all over the place - on street corners as well as in the opera house. Viva Verdi! was not just shouted to support the opera composer. It stood for Viva **V**ittorio **E**mmanuele **R**e **D'I**talia. Sympathetic Liberal opinion, including Verdi's, hoped to make King Victor Emmanuel of Piedmont the Monarch of a united Italy, combining all the minor Dukedoms and Principalities into one state. Neapolitans were not impressed.

Verdi wove political comment and liberal ideas into his romantic dramas. His melodies, plots and stage craft appealed to Italians in the age of Cavour and Garibaldi. His patriotic chorus for Scottish exiles in *Macbeth* was heard as a lament for the exiled Italians of the time, and for those suffering under Austrian occupation.

So too was his Chorus of Hebrew Slaves in *Nabucco*. It is now used as a national anthem by the Northern League for their hoped-for independent state of Padania lying in the Alps of northern Italy.

I stopped at a cool, scrubbed *Osteria* alongside a Wine Bar in one of Barga's many tiny squares that have not yet been taken over by the Frappucino and Eggnog Latte brigade. It had once been a chemist's shop – now it's a front line eatery. It served anchovies, lard toast, mountain ham and other local finds.

Every year, little by little, an unspoilt new *Trattoria* appeared out of the shadows, and culinary hopes were lifted again.

Next to the offices of the Mountain Club of Garfagnana I sped an Opera Barga Poster extolling the summer's musical events. For Music and Mountains are what Barga is all about. I edged in to the Opera Office. The walls were lined with some remarkable sketches of stage sets and costume designs – with that ethereal feel of 'Gone with the Wind'. They were the work and brainchild of an Anglo Saxon love affair with Italian Theatre.

In the post-war recession, two budding Italophiles, Gillian Armitage and Peter Hunt pitched up from England. She was a costume and set designer in the heydays of British Theatre and Cinema. Pinewood, Elstree and Denham were her hangouts. It was short lived romance. She forsook the declining British film industry, ridden with trade union restrictions, and arrived in Italy with her actor-director husband Peter. They had found a treasured corner of unspoilt Tuscany with mountains and music. And a real challenge. For Barga boasted a derelict little gem - an ancient Opera House. They launched a school for young actors and musicians. During many summer evenings the open squares around the sombre historic centre were brought to life, and resounded to the musical success of their enterprise. The Opera Barga Festival was born.

The modern day Jazz Festival evolved alongside the more classical Opera Festival. Today, the renaissance theatre and the haunting squares resound to more Trad Jazz than Ancient Arias.

Through the years, the local community restored the Opera House. It had started life as the *Teatro dei Indifferenti* - Theatre of the Indifferent Ones. Then it became the hang-out of the Different Ones - the Elite of Barga. Such was the city's fame on the musical map that Puccini's Madam Butterfly was first staged here at the same time as La Scala in Milan, in February 1904. Then it stood empty and forlorn for years. It was a challenge. With the help of local grants and donations from the EU, the tradition of musical harmony was revived.

The Hunt legacy lives on. They delve into the Vatican archives to find unexplored masterpieces never before performed. And to keep the novelty alive, many another hardly heard *Bel Canto* is played out in this gem of an Opera House with the perfect acoustics. There are three tiers of boxes around the perfectly spaced auditorium.

I joined Angela and Inge in a Box big enough for 3 slim chairs. The girls were squeezed on either side of me. I pushed my seat back to the wall and faced the music. We were so hemmed in, that neither us, nor them, could see or be seen, from either above or below.

A pair of elegant legs propped themselves up against the balustrade and my thighs, gently caressing me through linen slacks. On the other side of me, equally endearing movements were tenderly working their magic through my arms, in time to the music. Something stirred in me. Yet the music was mindless. It's hard to find a more truly boring piece, than *Lacryma,* or Tears, by Benjamin Britten. The 20 minutes passed as slowly as a visit to the dentist. I fell asleep, thinking I was watching a Ballet.

When I awoke from my siesta, I am lying on another balcony. The girls are reclining in the sun. We are perched on the precipice of a real old *Rustico*, looking down the valley towards Lucca. The distant clouds, rolling over the hills, make an inspiring operatic backdrop to the working farm below. The air is limpid, saturated with the buzz of insects, and the sound of Barga's bells above.

Call it economy of sound. To the uninitiated, it still takes a lot of grey matter to work out this simple code. The hour bell only tolls to a maximum of six strikes. It then starts at one strike again. 7 o'clock in the morning or evening is therefore one solitary BOING. 8 o'clock is two BOINGS, and so on, up to 12 midday or midnight which is six BOINGS. They rarely wake you at night, but toll on certain days at 4 o'clock to wake you from Siesta. Bing Bang Bong in quick succession, or 'God Bless You', rings out across the valley on Feast Days.

Below us dangles an erringly steep vineyard running down the hillside. One side is dominated by the grey stones walls of the town, with its Cathedral pinnacle. The other escarpment is dotted randomly with stone farmhouses and red tile roofs.

We are overlooking one of the last real contadini farms in the area.

"Mina, Mina, Giuseppina!" cries the lady from next door. I can't quite work out who she's calling. Is it her cat or her hens? I watch as a speckled 'all-sorts' stalks up to the hen coop with Tuscan feline finesse.

"Vieni su !, Vieni su !" cries her husband from far down below us. He peers up through the terrace of ripened vines looking for the hens. With a long knurled stick he hits the side of the hen house: "Thwack". A mortified Giuseppina holds her ground. The hen refuses to budge, leave alone bed down for the night.

"Thwack" the long bamboo pole reaches up again into the vine trellises. This time a flurry of feathers appear. Three or four hens flap from nowhere. They flutter up, squawking madly. Giuseppina watches defiantly from the roof of the hen house. Three quarters of an hour later, before night materialises, they settle down.

The man of the mountains knows his hens better than the back of his time-worn hands. He is one of the last of the sun weathered farmers, who like generations before him, has worked these fertile valleys. Engaging in the strenuous and eternal work of the landscape that has kept them happy and stress free. That's why they all live so long in these parts.

Afterwards we go down to his cellar and share a good glass of wine. "This is back breaking work," he indicates, as he rubs his back.

He makes a good glass of wine. Absolutely no artificial chemicals or manures are used in production, with only the barest minimum of fungicide spray on the grapes. The variety is a mystery - somewhere between a local hybrid and a Sangiovese - the oldest grape variety used by the Romans and the Etruscans. It looks, and tastes, more like a sun ripened all sorts of biodynamic proportions. The same variety that starry eyed modern winemakers now charge a fortune for, under the pretence of having created a lunar miracle. For them the moon is everything. The weeding and pruning of the vineyard, the selection and picking of the grapes is all dictated by the timing of the planets around the sun. According to these fringe experts, the wine is only transferred in cellars beneath the earth, when the heavenly conditions prevail. Bi-polar conditions prevent Trauma - at a trendy price. And the wine only lasts as long as the skies are clear of meteors.

In these back wooded hills there are no such modern secrets. The grapes are tested for ripeness by the smell, and the feel and texture of the sugar content. They are collected and pressed in an antique wooden cask. Then the juice is vatted and left to mature. The glass bottles are sterilised only with boiling water. Hardly any sulphur is used.

I watch as he takes down a bottle from the shelf. Floating on the top of the wine, in the neck of the bottle, is a thin layer of pure vegetable oil - to keep the air out. With a deft skill he sucks through a straw. A flick of the wrist throws off the last splodge of oil. He pours me a glass. *Delicioso!* Fresh as a berry from the sun laden vine.

This is a healthy land. Arthritis is unheard of. It isn't just the red grapes and wine, or the local spelt which was food for the Romans. The *Mangia Fagioli* - the Bean Eaters of Tuscany - are the least knarled of all. Twisted finger joints just disappear after years and decades of eating beans - packed with miraculous Soya.

Across the valley a shotgun shatters the afternoon peace. The hunters are on the prowl, for blackbirds, thrushes, robins or anything else that moves too slowly to avoid these trigger happy sportsmen. National laws mean nothing. Local laws override them. Nasty traps still abound. Bird inspectors get stabbed, shot at, and slashed with sickles as they stand their ground against this carnage.

The new industrial revolution has arrived. The buzz of asthmatic Apies and the whiz of strimmers break the silence. The chorus continues with circular saws, electric clippers and chattering Chinese bargains. The noisy cavalcade is enveloped in a cloud of fumes - cutting, stripping, eroding and exploding the landscape. Sometimes causing landslides down the mountain.

We are a stone's throw from the Porta Macchiaia. – the imposing gateway which once kept the barbarian Luccans and Pisans at bay. The bells still toll the curfew hours. They ring out across the landscape for at least five minutes to warn that bandits and robbers may abound. Those unlucky ones who missed the curfew would scurry to safety in underground caverns with iron doors locked from the inside.

The horse drawn wagons would sidle up to the gate, jockeying for position to turn the last corner through the mediaeval archway with restricted access. Modern cars fare no better.

Like all city gates, each has a life of its own. It is a microcosm of village life. The Gatekeepers lodge was once Marisa's Bar and Grocery. One entrance stood inside, and the other entrance lay outside the city walls

One could buy the staple food, and sit on the roof with a spectacular view. Long ago they made the tables so small that the boisterous card players had to clear out. I dodged in for the odd coffee or glass of wine. I stood at the telephone, feeding it with a handful of Gettone - those groovy little discs which were the only means to make long distance calls. As I gazed down the road, I watched Father Renzo, the learned cleric hobble up the hill with a sturdy walking stick on his way to say Mass. Through the imposing old gateway he was joined by a chorus of barking dogs, as he stopped occasionally to draw breath. He was a man of few words or none, yet he greeted me reverently every day, with a severity that betrayed the kindness behind his reserved exterior. Then one day he paused and smiled. He had seen me go to Mass one Sunday morning, and had recognised that foreigners, especially Inglese, are not all heathens.

At the top of this street of the dumb and the blind stands a little church used on high days and holidays. The Fornacetta is where the Della Robbia brothers hung out with their famous furnaces. Luca della Robbia was employed as a boy on the Florentine bronze doors. He got bored. So he struck out on his own, creating bas-reliefs in marble and terracotta. He was mesmerised by the old Greek enamelware which gave him the idea for sculptures in relief. After numerous experiments he achieved near perfection in covering clay models with enamel, consisting of ingredients of glass, mixed with tin oxide. These were fired, amongst other places, in the Furnaces of the Fornacetta.

In these foothills of the Apennines the annual feast day of the local patron saint is reinforced by an

**LIBERTY STYLE ART DECO BUILDINGS ON THE SEA FRONT AT VIAREGGIO.** *PAGE 169*

**THE *LUNGARNO* OF PISA. ALONG THE ARNO FROM THE BALCONY OF THE HOTEL VICTORIA.** *PAGE 32*

**BAGNI DI LUCCA STATION. 3 MILES FROM THE SPA TOWN, BUILT IN EDWARDIAN TIMES.** *PAGE 50*

**THE DEVILS BRIDGE. BUILT IN THE ERA OF THE COUNTESS MATILDA OF TUSCANY.** *PAGE 51*

**RELICS OF RAIL TRAVEL AT PIAZZA AL SERCHIO, THE ONE TIME REMOTE TERMINUS IN THE LUNIGIANA WHEN THE RAILWAY ARRIVED IN THE 1930'S.** *PAGE 116*

**THE CHURCH OF ST GEORGE, TELLARO
ON THE GULF OF POETS, WHERE THE
GIANT SQUID GRABBED THE BELL ROPE
TO WARN OF SARACEN INVADERS.**

even trendier irreverent event. Not as controversial as the Feast of the Thrush, it is the *Sagra di Pesce e Patate* - The Feast of Fish and Chips. Just outside the city walls, the local football field is turned into a kind of Jubilee party. A jumbo feast under warm sunny skies is set along tables beside sturdy benches. It's a mass catering contract drummed up by Italian ingenuity - only this time it's of Anglo Saxon origin. Not long ago potatoes were unheard of in these regions. Rice from the north and chestnut flour from the local mills was the staple fare. So the enterprising emigrants who had prospered in Scotland, on ice cream and fish and chips, scored with their novel approach. The batter for frying was specially flown in from Glasgow, and so successfully did the festival take off, and so rich the revelry, that the city fathers moved the Feast of Fish and Chips to the local sports ground.

Many a Castelvecchi or a Moscardini chirps in with a lyrical reminder of his origin. For these Tuscan Hills are indeed alive to the sound of rolling R's and K's. It is the broad Garfagnana-Glaswegian accent. Sometimes it's a reassuring Godsend. Other times it's over indulgent. It's rarely over the top, because it's part of the landscape, like a call to the ancient gathering of the clans.

Even the Giovanni Pascoli was struck by it:

**"Between the sounds of bagpipes I heard the sound of lullabies..."** [3]

Suddenly, out of the blue, comes the time of reckoning. Of all pious processions, we find ourselves involved in one with real, down-to-earth meaning. It only happens once in a while. Most Festa's are annual affairs. The largest and longest is for St Christopher, the patron saint of travellers, who vies with St Rocco, the patron saint of Doctors. Barga takes both her saints seriously, in carnival combinations of religious ceremony and mediaeval pageant.

In stark contrast, a peaceful demonstration against the closure of the local hospital is a rarer, more solemn occasion. It is a dignified gathering, enfolding man's destiny through the miracles of modern science.

The procession begins at the Franciscan monastery next door to the hospital. It struggles up the hill, like the climb to Calvary. We dodge around the city walls to meet it, as it proceeds through the narrow gap of the Porta Reale, the Royal Gate of King Victor Emmanuel - once overlooked by the long suffering Cedar Tree. In front, a shiny new Police car moves at a snails pace, amber lights twinkling in harmony to the drum beats. It is a funereal procession. A banner is carried, like a token gesture of Trade Union solidarity, symbolising the power of the local health service. It is borne with a flourish of regimental pride, and with life-threatening theatrical meaning. The statue of St Francis follows, carried shoulder high by 4 hardy Barghigiani - pursued by Franciscan Friars.

Two slim-line police girls in uniform follow, their hair hanging from their unisex caps. No space for sex discrimination here. They beckon with their hands to the keep the crowd from spilling into the street. Almost immediately behind, the real procession begins. The Church's influence is apparent. A cross bearer carries a rustic giant crucifix. Then follow the Nuns and

Monks in robes. Then the priests of the diocese.

The redoubtable Father Renzo hobbles along gamely in the middle of this ecclesiastical melee. His walking stick hits the cobblestones with a rhythmic beat. There is hardly a sound except the tap tap, and the distant drum beats. He makes a poignant gesture, almost as if the wants to make a statement on his own declining health.

Through the airless summer night an alter-boy carries a wooden pole. Attached to the top are two incongruous loudspeakers. He carries a massive battery belt around his waist, which weighs him down in heavy penance.

A microphone wire trails behind him, attached to which is the Parish Priest. All of a sudden: "Ave Maria Grazia Plena" is intoned. It echoes out through tinny woofers. The whole procession and bystanders respond in chorus: 'Dominus Tecum'. They mumble, and fumble and bumble along.

"AVE MARIA Grazia Plena" the loudspeaker reverberates louder, and more menacingly. Then the tone changes. "Madre del Dio, Madre Simpatica, Madre Immaculata, MADRE DOLOROSA" he cantillates reverently, fidgeting wildly. The Monsignor who follows him is expert at dignified ceremony. With eyes straight ahead, he is escorted by two smart acolytes holding candles. Another fierce looking individual carries an incense burner, exuding fiery streaks as he swings it grimly. The crowd cross themselves again.

Mayor, Councillors and dignitaries stroll on silently, mollified by numerous Hail Mary's.

The mob follows, mouthing the responses in

unison, and fading away as the loudspeaker disappears further and further, winding relentlessly up the hill inside the city walls. Almost the entire town turns out, either to watch or to walk. Children holding candles march side by side with old men. It has certainly encouraged individuals of the fair sex. They are nearly all old women. Others of not such religious zeal dawdle along at the very end. They wind relentlessly upwards and onwards towards their goal - the Cathedral at the top of the hill, mirroring the Tuscan idea of the endless cycle of life, where there is light at the end of the tunnel.

The Hospital is saved.

[1] I Stood Tiptoe – John Keats
[2] The Hour of Barga – The Songs of Castelvecchio. G. Pascoli.
[3] The Bagpipes – The Songs of Castelvecchio. G. Pascoli.

(Authors Translations)

# Chapter 5

# BARGA BATTLES

~~~~

It is not difficult to see why Barga was fought over for so long. Lucca, Pisa and Florence had a bash at it. Even the far-off Milanese wrestled for its rich pickings. Everyone took a shine to its prosperous trading links. Its true independent spirit did not just survive – it thrived; with reserved aloofness.

The grand old Countess Matilda of Tuscany, who owned a valuable slice of Italy, started the ball rolling. 700 years ago she combined the boldness of Queen Boadicea with the brains of Queen Victoria.

She owned a valuable slice of Italy, and arranged the first of many tax free privileges that put Barga and its commerce on the map. When she died, she left all her lands to the Church. Lucca thought this was stretching the imagination too far, especially since Barga was in Lucca's own back yard and a long way from the Papal States across the mountains. The warriors of Lucca set off up the mountain. They were the first people to use Hand Cannons, loaded with stone balls, and fired from the shoulder. As they went on the march, their claim was encouraged by their recalcitrant local Bishop. On the way up through the Serchio River Valley they seized castles and churches. When they reached Barga they stopped. The Castle was occupied by the Papal Nuncio, sent by the Pope to keep a beady eye on the area, and report back about all this skulduggery. Fearing the wrath of God, they shied off. Barga then threw in its lot with the rich rival Pisans – and finally with the even richer Florentines.

An uneasy truce prevailed. The Garfagnana once more prospered as a trading region. Along well-worn mule tracks, merchants came to buy wool, silk, sheep's cheese, lamb, honey - and even marinated trout from the Serchio River. Barga was coining it, and Florence was wallowing in it. Their jealous rivals did their best to stop them in their tracks. In return, Barga started smuggling over the mountains, avoiding Lucca like the plague.

Florence, finally bought the town in 1341. However, before the ink had tried on the receipt for a Hundred Thousand Gold Florins, Pisa pitched in. They sent up troops, and although they grabbed the surrounding villages, they never managed to subdue prosperous Barga, surrounded by stout mediaeval walls.

*Florens Ensis* - the Flower of Cities - had retained a premium prize. She became mistress of Tuscany, from the hills to the plains, by sheer strength of her citizens. Tied to Florence, Barga Fiorentina became a stronghold of the Medici's. Huge tax exemptions followed. There was no stamp duty on Contracts; no Millstone, Tobacco or Salt tax. A Bank was founded, and a Playing Cards factory opened up for exports. When Gunpowder tax was reduced, Arsenals opened up along the river valleys. Exemption from Leghorn Tax on the coast allowed free trade with other nations, because Leghorn – *Livorno* - was the sea port for Florence. Under the benevolent gaze and religious liberalism of the Medicis, Leghorn flourished on trade both legal and illegal.

Like all things Tuscan, this was a land of extremes. Fascism was born across the surrounding mountains in Emilia Romagna, and Barga became as enamoured as anywhere else with the ideals of Mussolini. They remembered his visit in 1930 when he came to power. He gave Barga the status of 'City', in return for having made him an honorary citizen. He also gave the struggling local people ample food and good advice on reconstruction and development. He encouraged the young. By following him, they had nothing to lose and everything to gain.

Unfortunately he backed the wrong horse. When Italy was occupied by the Germans during World War II, this area was the sharp edge of the Gothic Line. Along this fortified boundary bitter memories prevailed. The Apennines and Apuan Alps were the scene of raging conflicts between scattered clandestine guerrilla forces, and ruthless counterinsurgency forces made up of German and Fascist units. They threw away the rule books to stamp out the partisans. A ten to one ratio of reprisals was a 'normal' atrocity.

We were sitting in the genteel Alpino Hotel and Restaurant, which was once the local headquarters of the German High Command. Today, all sorts of lovely ladies take tea, cakes and aperitifs at the pavement tables, whilst the old men recall the past, arguing, or nodding off under the shadow of the Cedar tree.

It reminded me of the Tree of Idleness, that 200 year old mulberry tree under which Lawrence Durrell wrote 'Bitter Lemons', in that remote sleepy square of Cyprus half a century ago. He was warned that the tree's shadow 'incapacitates one for serious work'. For it is only around old trees that life stagnates. When Barga's ancient Cedar, which overlooked the Royal Gate, went into terminal decline, life drifted down to the younger one - in this new part of town. Here, at the crossroads, cars surround it. Bars overshadow it. Six banks emanate from it. Grocery shops flourish on the doorstep. Along the wall, beside the bus stop, sit the old codgers, silently watching Barga go by.

Some of them remembered wars of more recent times. The Ice Cream Wars of the early 1980's were waged between the local ice cream makers of Glasgow and the expatriate citizens of Barga.

Italians like the Marchettis had migrated to Scotland with their ice cream business. According to the local opposition they had muscled onto disputed territory. Vendors vans were attacked, and shotguns fired into windscreens, in an effort to scare away the 'intruders' and retain a monopoly. This was not just lucrative for ice creams, but for selling drugs and stolen goods. Violence and intimidation continued, until one day a van driver for the Marchetti's was targeted. His family flat was doused with petrol and set on fire. Six members of the Doyle family died in the flames.

It all ended when a Glaswegian ruffian named Campbell – new to the ice cream game – and his henchman Steele were convicted of murder. They were sentenced to life in prison. The legal fight continued for another 20 years, when they won their appeal for release under strange circumstances.

We sat inside the restaurant. I was with Angela and Inge, who being Austrian, was in pilgrimage mood. Against the other wall, alone, sat a foreign girl, in her thirties. We got chatting. She spoke a little English, good Italian, and surprisingly better German. I guessed, correctly, that she was from Bolzano on the Italian-Austrian border – an area which still considers itself part of the Austro-Hungarian Empire. I said to her that the war was really here - on this doorstep.

"Oh yes", she replied matter of factly, "*La Linea Gothica*. My father was also here - in an Austrian Regiment. He had fought to the end across the very north of the Gothic line, and had been captured by the Americans."

She was keen to see where it all happened. Her knowledge surprised me. She leant across and spoke to Inge in German. Perhaps she too was in pilgrimage mood, to lay things to rest.

"Bad things were done on both sides. In war all things happen" interrupted a perceptive Italian, in excellent English, as he gesticulated from across the next table.

He could see I was uncomfortable, so he added with diplomatic dignity:

"Too much time has passed to be angry".

I guessed his Italian directness was aimed at me, to avoid what is perceived in Italy as the Anglo-Saxon hypocrisy of false politeness. He shrugged his shoulders as only an Italian can shrug off close memories of a Civil War. For some it is still too close to talk about. Many forgive, but nobody forgets.

I felt I was trespassing on delicate and

sometimes disputed ground. For this subtle shift of "re-writing history" has given an *equivalenza* to both partisans and fascists. Some argue that they were both legitimate Italian patriots in a mindless conflict. Modern right-wingers strongly identify themselves with the anti-communist era of Mussolini, often too readily glossing over the draconian Nazi-Fascist atrocities.

A generation ago people were hiding in the mountains, dying in the streets and being deported to who knows where.

Having listened, I had glimpsed through my own eyes the two worlds that made up theirs.

For it was in these very hills above us that one of the fiercest skirmishes on the Gothic Line took place. The Battle of Sommocolonia - Boxing Day 1944.

The Serchio Valley was the scene of heavy bombardments from both sides. Defiantly standing above Barga, with a back drop of the Apennines, is the little mediaeval hilltop hamlet of Sommocolonia. A cluster of simple stone houses was named by the Romans *Summa Culonia* - the highest outpost. It was a strategic sight, looking down toward the Serchio River and the hill approaches on three sides. On Christmas Day 1944 two platoons of American soldiers of the Buffalo Division had taken up positions in the hamlet. That night, 600 soldiers of the crack veteran Austrian-German Mittenwald Battalion, guided by local Italians of the fascist Black Brigade, as well as Italian and Austrian Alpine troops, approached the strategic hamlet along the ridge of mountains. Throughout the night, hundreds of these troops entered the hamlet dressed in ordinary clothes. At day break most of them changed into their uniforms. The defensive band of 60 American men had been joined by a score of valiant local partisans. They fought desperately to repel the invaders who were swarming in. Their task was complicated by the presence among the Germans of Italian soldiers still dressed as partisans The force drove the Americans and real partisans back into the centre of the village. Desperate fighting occured, from house to house. Door to door carnage followed. In hand to hand combat, the Partisans were surrounded in the narrow streets and alleys of this tiny hamlet. One was caught in an upstairs room and thrown from the second floor window to the rocks below. His body was left with American cigarettes and chocolate, planted in his hand.

In the heat of battle, one of the local residents came out of his house to escape the inferno. Seconds too late in putting up his hands, he was mowed down with volleys of machine gun fire. Others were killed by artillery fire.

All nine Partisans who were killed were young lads aged between 19 and 25. Some were local boys; others came from across the mountains in Modena.

Of the sixty Americans, some retreated down the mountain. Of those left, 15 were killed.

Lieutenant Fox, with an observer, remained on the second floor of the highest house on the summit of the hamlet, directing fire from the artillery across the valley. As the enemy closed in, he realised the hopelessness of the situation. He called on his radio for fire, increasingly close to his strategic position - even though there would have been ample time for him and his observer to escape before the enemy came beating

101

at the door. One of his last instructions, whilst the enemy were swirling round the building and already on the first floor, was to call for fire on his position. "That last round is just where I want it. Bring it in 16 more yards," he called over the radio. When this was queried by the artillery commander: "Confirm, confirm your position!" Fox demanded: "Fire! There are more of them than there are of us. Put fire on my OP!" (Observation Post). 12 further rounds of high explosive hit their target. The entire building was destroyed, instantly killing Fox and his aide, together with numerous enemies.

It was one of the more heroic actions of the American 'Buffalo' Division. This was the last segregated all black US Army division, and the only black division to fight in Europe during World War II. Their name emanated from the rampaging actions against Indian tribes in the early days of the American mid west, when they were named Buffalos after the fearsome animal herds. There was a certain circumspect look at the behaviour and steadfastness of these raw coloured recruits, yet 13,500 of them gained their share of victories in war-time Europe under conditions which few others were expected to meet.

Lieutenant Fox was recommended posthumously for the Distinguished Service Cross. Nearly 40 years later, in 1982, this was confirmed and awarded to his widow.[1]

In the war in Italy, estimates of active Resistance ran to as many as 350,000 partisans and patriots who were fighting with little direction. Tens of thousands roamed the mountains, or operated in towns.

In all, over 45,000 of them were killed. 21,000 were wounded.[2] Fighting as armed guerrillas mainly on the side of the Allies, they harassed and pinned down numerous German troops. Finding support, particularly in summer, they were not just disenchanted communists. They were a mixed band of anarchists, socialists, republicans, monarchists, atheists and Christians. Some were escaped or deserted soldiers still holding their weapons; others were against Mussolini's plans to conscript them. Yet the vast majority were united in fighting to rid Italy of German occupation and Fascist totalitarianism

In the three months of the spring and summer of 1944 the number of active, armed partisans increased three-fold.

Under guidance of British and American SIS, scores of Italian Americans were eventually drafted in behind enemy lines to reorganise and work with the partisan units. By December 1944, 17 secret radio transmitters were operating in northern Italy, supplying daily intelligence reports on troop movements, military installations, bomb damage, counter intelligence data and psychological warfare aids, as well as coordinating drop zones for the re-supply of armed partisan groups.

"The Americans bombed all the bridges over the River Serchio – except the Devil's Bridge – which was just wide enough to allow a jeep to cross".

I was talking to the local estate agent. His father was born in Tuscany. His mother hailed from the Emerald Isle.

"My parents home was occupied by the both the Germans, and then the Americans. The German

Officers took their boots off. The Americans waded in. They trod all over the place, planting their muddy feet on sofas and chairs".

"The Germans behaved like gentlemen. That is the ordinary Army ones", added his cousin. "My mother was here too. A kindly German Officer of the old school told her: The SS are coming up from the coast. Get away - as fast as you can. Stay indoors – or anywhere to avoid them".

Today, a German girl, married to a local Italian, lives down the road. She went back to Germany for a life threatening operation. After months of recuperation she came home to Italy. To her great astonishment she saw that her garden had been planted with 21 Olive trees by her neighbours.

This silent symbol of longevity brought more joy and gratification than any kind words. It was an endearing gift of Italian appeasement with genuine life-giving meaning.

[1]  **Buffalo Soldiers in Italy**. Hondon B. Hargrove.
[2]  **Italy's Sorrow**. James Holland.

# Chapter 6

## LUNIGIANA

Summer was reverberating with a languid bang when I dropped off at Castelnuovo. I was kicking my heels, waiting for Angela and Inge to catch me up.

We were on our way over the mountains, by train to the coast. This laborious trek, up the hills and down the dales to the sea, carves through the edge of the Apennines.

As I hit Castelnuovo the annual preparations for the *Festa* were well in hand. The streets were ringing to the sounds of hammering. Wooden stands were being erected on scaffolding for the coming merry-making. Plastic bunting in brash gaudy colours, along with the stylish shades of modern Italy, zig-zagged across the streets from the lampposts. It wasn't just the patriotic green, white and red of Italy, but also the red white and blue of France and Britain. The European community concurred at this mountain extremity.

I weaved my way through this mind-boggling gauntlet, treading carefully past tables laid along the pavements outside the shops. I ducked down an alleyway at the end of the street, as I spied a not-so-busy haven of tranquillity. It appeared to have been - once upon a time, a classic old fashioned gem of an *Osteria*. Now it was a 'Bar' pure and simple. The *Festa* had passed it by, nicely, I thought. Yet in more ways than one, as it turned out, time had stood still for this little treasure tucked away in an almost forgotten corner of a remote extremity of Tuscany.

When I entered, the owner was lounging behind the bar. He was middle aged, moustachioed and friendly.

I perched on a rickety stool and settled down to consider my bearings. Two garrulous men were noisily sipping coffee in the corner. They turned, and attempted to tell me something in the local lingo. They soon gave up.

It was strange to see a bar run entirely by a man in this matriarchal society in the mountains. For it is only in Italy, and only an Italian who can achieve that sublime masculine ideal, or rather contradiction, of expression and apparent submission.

We struck up a conversation in Pidgin English and rustic Italian. Mario appeared to be a man of pure local mountain descent. He had toiled away – or perhaps idled away - religiously every day since his parents had died. They had left him to ponder over this tidy little inheritance in the centre of town.

In a sober way, Mario's bar was as colourful as the man himself. I looked around. Every kind of bric a brac was in evidence. Chianti flasks hung alongside Scottish tartan mugs and mountain deer horns of the hunter variety. British Bulldogs and Horse Brasses stood together with crossed spoons and giant swords of the Gaelic variety. He had copied some of his ideas from British pubs, I guess, even though he had probably never set foot in England. His choice reflected what appeared to me to be his credo that, in this part of Italy at least; all Brits were of Gaelic origin. Yet nowhere did I see any of the kind of overloaded Kitsch which would have put it on the tourist map. It was all old fashioned humbug which somehow blended into the landscape.

The sounds of the *Festa* preparations were going on outside. I asked him whether there was anywhere to stay around these busy parts. *"Qualcosa semplice"* – 'somewhere simple to sleep', I suggested, rubbing by thumb and forefinger together in a sign of pecuniary pessimism – Italian style. In response, he rubbed his hands with glee and pointed out of the window down the road. *"Si, in fondo - La Locanda!"*

It stood at the bottom of the street. A rusty metal sign hung over a cul-de-sac alleyway, spelling out in brash, cut-out letters the word: *Locanda* - a loquacious word which describes an Inn, a Lodging house or a Rest house. Much more simple than an Osteria, and not as grand as an Albergo, a Locanda is the sort of place that must have stayed open late at night for weary travellers scurrying into the walled cities as the curfew sounded.

The door slammed shut behind me, as I walked straight into the dinginess. It looked like the place had already packed up for the winter. Or forever.

"A simple room for the night?" I asked. *"Con tre letti.* With three beds!" The middle aged lady looked at me quizzically with detached astonishment. Then she called her sister. From behind the kitchen door the equally sprightly twin sister arrived. They both smiled. They can't say 'No' here, I thought. How nice. Then I discovered. No food. No hot water. Then the electricity was turned on in the bar. Coffee is about to be brewed. Judging by the size and shape of the archaic espresso machine, it was one of the original Gaggia's, invented long before the war. It was all decked out in shiny copper valves, handles and pressure dial attachments. After much reluctant hissing and spitting steam, the two sisters eventually got it going. It finally forced out enough energy to make the 'Espresso of the Century'.

For a moment, I wondered why Mario across the road had not joined forces with this sprightly pair to form a tidy little monopoly of Bar and Albergo in this charming little corner of Castelnuovo.

I looked around to find a stool which wasn't piled up on scrubbed wooden tables. Something in the corner stirred. Slumped in an easy chair, I spied a very old lady. She was quiet, still and comfortably ensconced in her *chaise longue* - covered in a blanket. I took her to be a permanent resident. She was a woman of great age and dignity; almost aristocratic looking. Perhaps their mother, I thought. She neither spoke, nor drank, nor smoked. I got the impression she hardly moved; except, I guessed, for meals, and a relapse again into the armchair. There was a battered television in the corner, spewing out Spaghetti Westerns of uncertain quality and sanity - from who knows where, into these remote Tuscan mountain extremities.

I spoke to her. I thought that a controversial approach to such a distinguished old lady would deserve a deliberated response. *Ricorda La Guerra?* I asked coolly. Do you remember the war? A fatuous question. She uttered some spitting expletives, which I was unable to translate. Then she launched into a muttering tirade about the *Tedesci* and the *Partigiani,* and the *Cretini* and the *Bastardi* - and the rest of the folk. I think she assumed I was German.

I looked across the room to refresh my mind. There on the wall was an exotic faded black and white photograph of a luxury liner sailing forth into some unknown sunny destination. Below it was written blandly in English: The Arandora Star - 15,000 tons - lost at sea July 2$^{nd}$ 1940.

"I know that ship, the Arandora Star. I remember her well" I exclaimed. "My Aunt and Uncle and their young son, sailed on her to South America just before the outbreak of war. I have a similar photograph at home".

She announced coldly, in perfect English: "My husband was drowned on it. With eight hundred others. We were living in Glasgow at the time". She spoke with a proud Scottish accent. "A few days after Italy declared war against Britain, the Police arrived on our doorstep. He was taken away to be interned. We were never told where he was going".

The Arandora Star was the proud flagship of the Blue Star Line. It was a sleek cruise liner designed to carry 350 first class passengers to exotic tropical destinations in the heady days of the 1930's.

At the outbreak of war she was painted in battleship grey and used as a troopship. Hardly a week after Mussolini had joined forces with Hitler in June 1940 every Italian man in the British Isles between 16 and 70 was declared an enemy alien. 'Collar the Lot', Churchill famously and fatuously declared. And they were. Hoteliers and Restaurateurs, Waiters, Engineers, and Film Directors – many of them retired. Some had been living in Britain for many years, mostly in Scotland.

The Arandora Star left Liverpool for Canada in high summer, overloaded with 734 Italian internees, 479 German internees and 86 German prisoners of War, as well as 374 military guards and crew. She bore no Red Cross markings or other identifications that she was a non-belligerent vessel.*

75 miles beyond Bloody Foreland, off the northern coast of Ireland, a German U boat, limping back home to Germany, fired her last remaining torpedo at the liner.

It made a direct hit on the engine room. All the men below decks were either drowned or killed in the blast. The turbines and generators were out of action and all communication was lost. The wireless room just managed to send an SOS message which was picked up by Malin Head Radio. Half an hour later the liner sank.

Of 14 lifeboats, 5 were destroyed or sank. Virtually all the life rafts, still lashed to the decks, went down with the ship. The boats were overcrowded with scores of internees climbing down the side ladders from the ship.

*Probably pointless. In January 1944, two days after the Anzio landings south of Rome, 3 Hospital Ships - brightly illuminated with large Red Cross markings - were attacked by the Luftwaffe. The 'St David' sank within a few minutes. Out of a total of 226 medical personnel and patients there were 130 survivors including 2 nurses.

The crew, together with a captive senior German Naval Officer who had taken charge, urged the many reluctant internees with lifejackets to jump in the sea and swim away to avoid the vortex of the sinking ship. Many refused, because they could not swim.

At 7.20 am, 35 minutes after being torpedoed, she rolled over, flung her bows vertically in the air and went to the bottom, carrying 805 with her.

As she went down, the Captain and his senior officers walked over the side as the water came up to meet them.

I looked back at the picture on the wall. Below the image, the list of family names lost in the tragedy read like the local telephone Directory.

Agostini, Alberti, Berttolini, Bertoncini, Biagi, Biagioni, Cardosi, Cosomini, da Prato, Filippi, Ghiloni, Gianotti, Humbert, Lucchesi, Moscardini, Piovano, Poli, Rochiccioli, Togneri.

Five were from Castelnuovo Garfagnana, eleven from Barga. Numerous others came from the surrounding villages and towns.

Most of the internees were elderly Italians, who had been resident in England and Scotland for many years. Some of course may have been Fascists. Many had joined the Party reluctantly.

"My husband wasn't a Fascist at all. It was purely a matter of social convenience to be one of them". The old lady looked at me for sympathy.

"The worst thing was we were never told where our husbands were going. Some couldn't swim. They were simple mountain folk, like my husband - brought up in these parts".

What had started in Britain as a sensible scheme to weed out enemy aliens had turned into panic reaction. More than anything else, the fiasco of the Arandora Star reversed this policy. No longer were internees sent to the Colonies. They were kept at places in the British Isles such as the Isle of Man.

History added an element of tragicomedy to this saga. Amongst the internees, there were supposedly two brothers who ran one of the smartest and most famous restaurants in London. One was short, fat and bald headed. The other was tall, slim and good looking. Neither of them could swim. The tall slim one supposedly saved himself from drowning by using his brothers' bald, bobbing head for buoyancy in the sea.

This was the myth surrounding the famous Quaglino Brothers; Giovanni and Ernesto, from Piedmont. They ran 'Quaglinos' - the most fashionable restaurant in London's West End in the 1930's. It was the favourite haunt of the Prince of Wales, and frequented by the 'café-society' of the day. On one occasion it entertained The Prince of Wales, King Alfonso of Spain and King Carol of Romania on the same evening. With the tact, charm and discretion of the finest Italian *maitre d'hotel* of his day, Giovanni 'Johnny' Quaglino handled this situation perfectly. In fact, he made everyone feel at home in his restaurant. It was rather like an old English drawing room in a rather grand house, where everything was rather mixed up and slightly shabby, like the aristocrats it mainly served.

The truth is that the Quaglino brothers were not on the Arandora Star. At the outbreak of hostilities, they chose to return to Italy, rather than be interned.

Ironically, on arrival in their homeland, they were incarcerated for their anti-Fascist views. With even greater irony, when the War ended, they had tremendous difficulty in obtaining permits to live in England. This started the rumour of their disappearance. It was only the intercession of Charles (later Lord) Forte which eventually facilitated their return to their famed London Restaurant.

I turned from the picture of the Arandora Star and changed the subject radically.

"What about the nearby railway" I suggested. She brightened up.

"I remember as a young girl when the railway arrived in the town, just before the First World War. It brought us prosperity. And happiness!"

She dozed off.

The railway was the key to opening up the Garfagnana. Mass migration and a backwater status had brought the locals to their knees. They were clamouring to be kept in touch with the cities below in the Tuscan plains and on the coast. In 1894 a few representatives of the Garfagnana region had pitched up at Castelnuovo to declare their annexation to Lucca, away from foreign influence. The schools were reopened, and plans for the railway were revived. There was a huge party in December 1894, and it seemed that something was about to happen. At last, work on the railway started, but little happened. It was going at a snails pace. Nearly ten years later it had barely got off the ground. Protests spread throughout the region and reached down the valley to the people of Lucca. Complaints became more vociferous and widespread. The railway had been promised, and talked about for too long. There were too many chiefs and not enough Indians. The entire Local Council of Lucca was dismissed.

Eventually enterprise triumphed. Heavy manual labour brought a certain detached relief when work commenced on the embankments, viaducts, bridges and cuttings. Yet there was still disagreement about the alignment. The surveyors were once again confronted with issues of cost cutting. The line followed the age-old route along the banks of the Serchio River, which at one time had been navigable the whole way through. Hugging the banks alongside the mule tracks, there was sometimes only a few feet between the river, the road and the railway. When the line reached the Devils Bridge it passed conveniently under one of the handy side arches.

Finally in the baking summer of July 1911, the line was completed. The first train puffed its way into Castelnuovo in a billowing white cloud, all the way from Lucca. Spewing forth smoke and steam, with thrusting crankshafts, it whistled and hooted its way forward to join in the wild celebrations on the edge of town. It put a lot of muleteers and wagon men out of business, and a lot more people into prosperity.

It was the beginning of a new era. Whilst the mule tracks stopped here, there was still a long way to go. Half a century passed before trains continued up the mountain.

Castelnuovo itself had a literary history. In renaissance times the Governor of Garfagnana was man of letters – a poet in fact. Ludovico Ariosto wrote the great romantic poem *Orlando Furioso*. This 40,000 line epic was a tale of knights in shining armour, of chivalry and romance, of witches, monsters and magic castles. He wrote it 'for the amusement and recreation of gentlemen, persons with sensitive souls, and ladies'. Being a man of letters Ariosto hated his official, yet well paid, job. "I'm not a man to govern other men", he wrote to his lover - as he collected taxes and kept the bandits, brigands and highway-men out of town for the Duke of Este.

Here, the Apennines stretch up to haughty snow-capped Alpine peaks. Mountain goats bleat, and cow bells tingle. Hard and soft cheeses mature together almost miraculously. And pigs produce ham almost as sweet as the Parma variety across the mountains in the province of Emilia Romagna. Through each valley, rivers feed into the Serchio, which winds it torturous way through a long winded route towards the sea, which is only twenty kilometers as the crow flies across the divide. Cypress trees get sparser and sparser as chestnut trees appeared on the landscape.

"I think Byron and Shelley were obsessed with sexual symbols – like Cypress Trees" chirped in Inge.

"Along with a death wish" added Angela, "Cypress trees only remind me of cemeteries".

Indeed, it is only in Tuscany that Cypress trees stand on their own, tall and proud – imposing phallic symbols in landscapes of unrestrained serenity. Long straight and hard, they are revered for their endurance. It gives them a kind of fertile immortality. Cypress wood was used for the arrows of Eros and the Staff of Hercules.

We rumbled on through the gold of the afternoon, edging across ravines, and sidling along sheer cliffs. We passed over ridges and bridges linking hilly villages to even loftier hamlets. In some places only a few empty houses stood by the rail side. Vines grew dangerously up to the edge of the line. The grapes were almost overhanging us as we whistled by. The trees changed from Chestnuts to Pine. As we drew up at neat little stations, pretty murals of local landmarks greeted us from the buildings. The stations were mostly deserted. At one wayside halt only a very old man, wearing a long ancient smock, stood watching and waiting. He stared at us, almost motionless, like a mediaeval dummy. Then he hitched up his trousers, scratched his head, and sauntered away abruptly, no doubt to while away the afternoon at other distractions.

Our iron horse struggled and squealed reluctantly to turn the tight corners, as we lurched into Piazza al Serchio. Here the two branches of the River Serchio meet, to form the crossroads of the route through the hills. One branch is born in the mountains towards the sea. The stronger branch is born in the equally high peaks which form the inland barrier with Emilia Romagna. The highest mountain in Tuscany, Monte Pisanino, 1946 metres above sea level, stands nearby.

It is a junction and a terminus all rolled into one, where the conductors greet each other and the train crews change. A loudspeaker thundered: *Terminato!*. *Terminato del treno*! All change. Out we scrambled - down onto the platform - like all continental ones built dangerously far below - designed for economy rather than agility. As the fat lady stumbled with her shopping bags, the smart conductor rushed off to refresh herself.

The hotel at Piazza al Serchio had a treat of a restaurant. Like many 'grand termini' the world over, railway travellers expected the best. We asked for a glass of the local wine at the bar. Politely served, we are reminded that there is a bar in the station nearby. "Siamo un ristorante!" We are a restaurant! She proudly proclaims. So we take the hint, and settle down for another smart, rural Tuscan feast in the mountains - a 3 course lunch for 8 euros, with a flagon of wine thrown in.

If the soul of a people is mirrored in the aroma and generosity of its cooking, this place excelled. We ate lashings of Carpaccio - thinly sliced raw beef. The deep red meat was a vivid reminder of the rich pigment used by the painter Carpaccio. We then ate mountains of home made Tortellini, thin with Sage and Pesto, dashed with butter. We finished with bottles of chestnut beer, brewed in these mountains. It was a wartime favourite – essential to survival.

Before the railway arrived in these areas, the only means of transport was either by ox-wagons dragged over rough, almost non existent roads, or by mule tracks that wound their way over each valley. In one respect, it is a world in which the railroad is an intrusion. Here, the pace of life still ambles on slowly.

We wandered about, aimlessly waiting for the next train to take us down the other side of the mountain towards the coast.

This is Lunigiana. The haunting area called the Mountains of the Moon by the ancient inhabitants of

117

Luni, far below on the sea, and famed for its outcrops of brilliant white marble - a foretaste of what was later discovered at Carrara.

Just after Piazza del Serchio we suddenly dart in and out of tunnels - more in than out. We thunder along, straight as a die, for nearly ten minutes through an 8 kilometer long cavern bored straight through the hillside. And then we spring into sunshine for a breather at Casola station. Almost immediately, we then plunge back into darkness again through another tunnel of 4 kilometers.

The railway is not far from the fascinating little town of Fivizzano, a few miles to the north. So once again we take a bus, this time lucky enough to catch one timed to go with the train's arrival.

Fivizzano was the ancient fortified capital of the region, standing out like many another Tuscan hill top town. We rambled into the main square across the river, and let ourselves out to explore and hunt for a thirst quencher. We came across what seemed to be the oldest and wisest *Albergo Ristorante Bar*, run by the same family since 1882. It wasn't easy to find a way in. A closed door from the street had no welcoming sign. But laughter and commotion from an upstairs window, gave the game away. The art deco rooms had elaborate ceiling lights, whilst family photographs decorated the walls. The restaurant was closed for the afternoon, but looked out onto a large rooftop, with a well watered garden, complete with a stone statue of Aphrodite at the Water Hole. Lurking in the vegetation among the pot plants was a real live Tortellini - a friendly shell shocked tortoise with a hole in his shell - the result of a bombing raid on Fivizzano in 1944. Although at least ninety years old, Toby was far from pensioned off. He was happily shuffling around as tortoises do, looking for vegetable scraps.

The train winds onwards between the Apennines and the Apuan Alps. Until the advent of the railway, this was remote territory. Two days travel from Lucca to Aulla is now achieved in two hours.

This unknown extremity, 'The Lost Corner' of Tuscany, is almost ignored. It is so remote that even some misguided maps of the region have chopped it off. A 'clenched fist' of mountainous land points up - further north than the latitudes of Genoa and Bologna. It is the sharp edge of the Apennines. And it was the sharp end of the War in Italy – the innermost regions behind the Gothic Line.

The villages of Vinca, Bardine San Terenzo and Castelpoggio suffered terrible reprisals under the Nazi occupation. Hundreds of residents were shot, burned or bayoneted. Their houses were torched with flamethrowers. At Bardine San Terenzo the SS tried to remove all the wine from the village cantinas. The partisans ambushed a German detachment on their way to the village, inflicting heavy casualties. Severe reprisals were ordered. The infamous one-armed Major Walter Reder arrived with his 'reconnaissance' group. They rounded up 107 local villagers, and shot them in batches. Old folk, women and children were mown down; one child survived by being covered by its mothers body. They trucked in 53 more men, from neighbouring areas and hung them with barbed wire. They announced that anyone who touched the bodies

119

would be shot. A courageous local lad defied the threat and buried nearly half of them. In counter reprisal, summary justice was meted out by the partisans against the Germans and local 'Black Brigade' Fascists. Individuals were hauled before people's courts and hastily formed tribunals.

To escape the onslaught from the coastal cities below, many had escaped up into these hills. When allied bombs destroyed much of Massa, 50,000 refugees fled up to the haven of these mountains, where the generous hospitality of locals saved them. The refugees swarmed into the countryside to forage. The local chestnut flour had fed not only the locals – but all and sundry - through the centuries. When chestnuts ran out, they lived on leaves or chestnut kernels. In the middle ages, two thirds of the bread in these hills and valleys was made from Chestnut Flour, ground in watermills on the rivers.

An Old Chestnut it may be - but in these parts, old wives tales have a twist of their own: 'Children are not found under a bush, they say, but in a hole in the chestnut tree'.

From here The *Marrons Glacé* of ultimate French fame spread down to Savona on the Liguria coast. This first brought them to the attention of the French who occupied Genoa in the late 1700's.

We lurched onwards, smoothly this time, down the mountain side, whooping in and out of more tunnels. The conductress in her sexy cap, slightly askew, wandered past us, for the last time. Carrying her airline-type hold-all, she was all prepared for a night stop at Aulla.

A sad city that has not regained its soul, Aulla was smashed to smithereens in the War. Scruffy and untidy, yet savagely defiant on the face of it, like the strategic English city of Slough, of which John Betjeman wrote: 'Come friendly bombs and fall on Slough - it isn't fit for humans now'.

At the time, the young Italian stationmaster at Aulla commanded the local partisan group. This was part of the Lunense Division, which included the Red Devils, *(Diavoli Rossi)* and the Justice and Liberty Battalion. It was a motley bunch of die-hards. One company even included escaped Russian prisoners and German deserters. This was quite normal for the war in Italy. They were well supplied and organized. From the hills surrounding the town, they fired a mortar shell onto an ammunition train standing in Aulla station, lying at the end of the single track up from the coast. In the massive explosion, virtually the whole town was destroyed. Only a few buildings, far from the railway station, were left standing. A group of over 600 Germans and Fascists from La Spezia, along with 150 local inhabitants, were killed. For days afterwards the unbearable stench of decomposing corpses was only staunched by carrying garlic cloves in the nostrils.

Around Aulla, several torrents join the mighty Magra River, which starts life as a bickering stream in the mountains 30 miles to the north. In the short distance past Aulla it races like a torrent to the sea. This is Malaspina territory; once a land of outlaws. With many of their 120 strategic castles still intact.

In the lower valley the river winds itself like a silver eel out of the Alpine atmosphere of the Lunigiana. It wasn't until the 1950's, long after the War ended, that the final leg of the railway from Lucca to Aulla was completed.

We took the train down towards the sprawling naval base of La Spezia.

Following the Magra River, we rumbled through another long winded tunnel straight as a die. On board there was now a happy holiday atmosphere. Away from the mountains we were joined by a noisy crowd of crusty business people, old ladies visiting relatives, shoppers, day trippers and school children. All turned their attention to the coming hustle and bustle of 'civilization' on the coast. There was a group of strident students sparkling with excitement, with white teeth rattling like pearls in the bright sunshine. One of them, a big girl with flashing dark eyes was showing off more than the others. She started to sing. The others followed, joining in perfect harmony as only Italians can. To my unmusical ears it wasn't a Neapolitan song, nor one I could easily recognize. It was a local Tuscan one. They sang on and on, changing tune in unison, led by the lead singer - the big dark girl. And then at the end, she suddenly fell asleep, as if intoxicated by her own melody. The abrupt silence turned into boisterous laughter as we neared the sea, and our journey's end.

# Chapter 7

## GULF OF POETS

~~~

From La Spezia Station, the trains amble up and down the coastal line to the north. The route rambles past the Cinque Terre - the only unspoilt spots on the coastline. In the summer months, these five little 'lost' fishing lands, ranged along the rocks, are only approachable by rail or boat. Chiselled into cliffs hanging precariously over the sea, the five beautifully remote villages, with their steep alleys and formidable approaches, romanticise this wild stretch of the Italian Riviera. It was once part of the Republic of Genoa's most inaccessible and dangerous possessions, when Barbary pirates roamed these shores.

In 1870, the new railway line bored through the cliffs, linking Turin and Genoa with the southern Ligurian coastal towns, and finally with Rome itself. It had been a hard slog, joining up a patchwork of divided regional railway companies in the squabbling Principalities, Dukedoms, Thrones and Dominations. Italy only became well and truly united in the 1880's.

I took the bus along the southern coastal route around the Gulf of Poets to meet Angela and Inge. The Bay of La Spezia is dominated by the huge sprawling port headquarters of the Italian Navy. As I zipped past docks, cranes and warehouses, I spied the pride of the Italian fleet.

On the bay, before I reached the little town of Lerici, I hopped off at tiny San Terenzo, where they were supposedly waiting. It was raining cats and dogs - a torrential unstoppable downpour brought from the Alps in the north.

The streets were empty; the hotels were full. The last one had one double room left - according to the proprietor. I told him my girlfriends were joining me later. He turned me away. When I stood outside, indolently gazing through the rain, and scrawling some angry notes for future reference, I realised why. They weren't interested in morals. They only wanted foreigners who did not come in from the streets dripping wet, to stay for one night only. What did they expect from roving Anglo-Saxons?

The girls phoned to say they were running late.

"According to the law we are in Liguria. According to our stomachs we are in Tuscany" explained a local San Terenzo gourmand, as he patted his belly.

Nowadays, this coastal area of Liguria is seeking a new home in neighbouring Tuscany, under an obscure law which allows transfer to another region for reasons of 'local identity'.

So although I was still in Liguria, I enjoyed the best of both worlds. I sampled a mixture of the local - as well as Tuscan food - to my hearts content.

I had stopped at one of the simple seaside restaurants, where the proprietor claimed to have worked in the Ivy Restaurant in London. Or was it the

Ritz or the Savoy? I know not what - the results were miraculous. That lovely Tuscan expression '*L'appetito vien mangiando* - The appetite is stirred by eating' broke my solitude. It was a Sunday, when the family feast is a sacred occasion. I sat on my own, surrounded by families of well behaved children and doting grandparents, nodding off at large tables. They turned to me as only polite Italians do, and offered me a taste of the numerous dishes that kept on appearing from the depths of the kitchen in huge steaming bowls. The famous *Tris*, - the trio of different kinds of pasta, appeared. There was the finest Angels Hairs Spaghetti, *Aglio and Olio*, simply made with golden Ligurian Olive Oil and fresh garlic. And of course, *Pesto Genovese*, made with pine nuts and basil from Genoa - just up the coast. And lastly - the one divine Spaghetti of all – *Frutta di Mare al Cartoccio*. Mixed seafood and shellfish, brought in on the fishing boats, is cooked with pasta in a foil bag, carried straight from the oven to the table. It is then opened out with its entire magnificent steaming aroma wafting under one's nose.

I remembered the dictum from Marcella Hazan: "Pasta can be one of the easiest dishes in the world to prepare. It is also one of the easiest to ruin."

Then I struggled to remember one of Sophia Loren's down to earth maxims: "Spaghetti can be eaten successfully if you inhale it like a vacuum cleaner".

The art of cooking is the art of seduction involving all the senses. It is the look and texture of the simple ingredients above all else. With the sound of sizzling … the aromas wafting from the pan … and the presentation at table. The whole joy of eating Italiano is in finding a *trattoria* where the food is as unspoilt as the prices. The simplicity of harmony and restraint makes Tuscan cooking the most sublime in the world – created like a work of art, or a classic melody in *divina proportione*. One simple dish, genuinely and amicably served, with pride, by a family with food in their hearts, is worth a thousand five star feasts.

"You have to be born into the art of cooking" concluded the exhausted restaurant owner.

I paid my compliments (and my bill), took my leave, and then snatched my siesta on the pebbly shore by the seafront. I removed the stones from the damp sand, made a nest, and dozed off, facing due west towards the restless waters from where the Ponente wind was brewing. Seagulls scorched overhead and dived further out to sea.

This Gulf of Poets was the gulf of free and urgent love, of wild dreams, and of youthful expression - chasing rainbows with tragic endings. It has remained through the centuries the magnet for writers and poets
.

**'Blessed shores, where love, freedom and dreams have no chains',** wrote Lerici's local poet Ceccardo Ceccardi.

One of a band of leading Ligurian poets of the 1900's, he was captivated by ageless beauty.

**'When we meet again, Time will have snowed Upon our heads, my love'.**

*Quando ci vedremo, Il tempo avra nevicato
Sul nostro capo, o amore*

126

When I awoke from my siesta, the waves were gently lapping at my feet. It had been an hour or more of sublime solitude. And the storm had passed.

The girls phoned me on my 'telefonino', unexpectedly early. It buzzed in my trouser pocket, like a symbolic new sex toy. Pleasure was in store. "Meet us later at the cafe by the boats, they said. "You'll find it by a snazzy little beach, somewhere beneath the caves of the Norman Castle at Lerici".

"I'll ring you when I find it", I replied, thinking of female navigational errors.

There was a gap in the storm, so I dawdled onwards, around the busy bay, past the *Casa Magni* at San Terenzo. It stands starkly on the overcrowded seafront with a plaque that marks the poet Percy Bysshe Shelley's two months sojourn here with his wife Mary, and Jane Williams, in their last abandoned *ménage a trois*. It was a shared posse of equality and friendship. Shelley was the prime exponent of that hippie philosophy which many women fail to understand. It worked on the basis that if you can't find everything in one person, you can find different people to provide all you are looking for in life. A community can give you what one individual cannot.

Mary Shelley tried to fathom out how a man can love a woman no less if he shares his love with another. She was driven to write 'Frankenstein' at the age of 22.

In 1822 the Casa Magni was the only half decent place available for the Shelley's to spend that tragic summer. The two storied villa was overhanging the sea, battered by the breakers, which - even in August, sometimes raged night and day. In those days, there was no road, only a rough footpath along the waterfront to Lerici.

Mary recalled: "The sea came up to the door and the wind was wild. The owner of the estate was mad. Even the locals thought so, since he had uprooted all the olive trees, and planted forest trees. Yet the scene was of unimaginable beauty. The blue extent of the waters, the almost landlocked bay, the near castle of Lerici standing to the east, and distant Port Venere to the west, with the Cinque Terre beyond. Sometimes the sunshine vanished when the Sirocco raged – the Ponente the wind was called on that shore. The howling wind swept round our exposed house, and the sea roared unremittingly. At other times sunshine and calm invested sea and sky, and the rich tints of Italian heaven bathed the scene in bright and ever varying tints.

"The locals were wilder than the place. Our near neighbours of San Terenzo were more like savages than any people I have before lived among. Many a night they passed on the beach, singing, or rather howling; the women dancing about among the waves that broke at their feet, the men leaning against the rocks and joining in their loud, wild chorus."

That summer was the happiest and most sublime ever for the beatnik poet, who would today have been inspired to write lyrics for pop songs. Percy recalled "I still inhabit this divine bay, reading Spanish dramas and listening to the most enchanting music. We have some friends on a visit to us, and my only regret is that summer must pass."

He lived a *louche* life on a frugal diet of grapes, raw eggs and vegetables. Apart from brooding on free love and revolution, messing about with boats was his other main distraction from poetry. His friend Edward Williams helped him. The sea was the pull; and it brought out the worst in him. In one of his darkest moments, Percy launched forth with Jane Williams and her children in a decidedly dodgy skiff. He drifted out to sea where he appeared to go into a trance. He teased her that the boat would tip, and proceeded to rock it. Terrified, she coaxed him back to shore and dashed into the waves with her children before the boat was beached, to escape his madness.

He had a habit of wandering around stark naked under the stars. He once appeared at the door, in the buff and dripping wet, to the astonishment of some visitors. Mary and Jane took it all in their stride.

The girls turned up, right on time, having also taken the bus from Lerici. They had propped themselves on the sea wall overlooking the shallow beach. We continued on our literary pilgrimage.

We meandered further along the road to Fiascherino, a remote seaside village jutting out into the bay from the rocky shore, well beyond Lerici. The late afternoon had an autumn feel, and something like the powerful 'Ponente' loomed ominously across the western waters. Light was fading in a molten haze, where the sea and sky were welded together, almost inseparably. Twilight was looming. Something was brewing. Behind us, the pale pink, cream, and terracotta houses blended eerily into the shadows. The windows were on fire, as the molten setting sun struck them. Impetuous waves resounded against the rocks. A few small wooden craft had been dragged high up onto the shingle beach of this tiny cove, shut in by rocks. The boats had been turned over, to reveal newly painted black, white, and vermilion bottoms, a vivid Mediterranean circus. The masts were neatly tucked away - safely stowed for the winter.

Nearly a century after the Shelley's had departed, little had changed in this tiny bay of Fiascherino. It was 1914, when the 28 year old son of a Nottingham coal miner, D. H. Lawrence, pitched up from England. He travelled along the twisty road from Lerici with his bride-to-be, Frieda Von Richthoffen. Eight years older than him, and already married with 3 children, she was the cousin of the Red Baron fighting ace from Silesia. She had lived in England and Germany, with divided loyalties. She was shortly to be divorced, and they married the following summer. They searched for peace - not only from the demoralising climate of World War I which was about to start. They came to escape the prying eyes and wagging tongues that had accused them of being German spies, and had eventually driven them out of Lawrence's home in Cornwall. When they finally left England in disgust, he had called it 'a banquet of vomit'.

This area was frequented by both British and German visitors of means, who entertained and lived in idyllic remoteness when Fiascherino was only a tiny hamlet on a windswept turquoise cove.

"There is a tiny bay half shut in by rocks and smothered by olive woods that slope down swiftly. You run out of the gate into the sea which washes among the rocks at the mouth of the bay. There is one pink, flat fisherman's house." Lawrence rented this four roomed cottage, perched just above a sea wall, bordering the sand and shingle beach. Access was either by small boat, or by scrambling down a steep path from the road.

"It is the most beautiful place I know," he wrote.

They lived on oranges and figs, and the occasional shellfish caught off the rocks from a rowing boat. Surrounded by olive groves and vineyards, the skinny, bearded prophet wrote that he was reminded constantly of the New Testament, and half expected to see Christ and his disciples wandering around the wilderness under the grey, light trees. An idyllic setting this was. It was Lawrence's attempt to recreate a lost paradise - an isolated, creative utopia where soul mates could eat, sleep and write. Yet they were often short of supplies. There was no real road - only a stone paved mule track which today is called the *Via Lawrence*, midway between Fiascherino and Tellaro. The only other way to Lerici was by slow boat around the coast to obtain food, mail and supplies. The Post was utterly unreliable. The manuscript for Lawrence's book 'The Sisters', was lost on its way from Munich to Lerici. It had been confiscated by the police in England, and banned. He began it again, and it turned out to be 'The Rainbow'. This was to be the first part of 'Women in Love'.

Here he first learnt to escape from the prison of his shut-in self, and was inspired to write of middle age wild abandon. He was obsessed with sex. "Most poets die of sex", he declared, "Keats, Shelley, Burns. Sexual frustration led to illness."

He was struggling with the Oedipus and other assorted emotional complexes. He was also doggedly determined to brave those difficult years of illness and rejection. Moral contradictions were the flavour of the month, and the aristocratic libertine Frieda - eight years his senior - was prone to prancing around, under sunny skies, in the buff. There were the inevitable conflicts, brooding rows which simmered on, reached a crescendo, and were finally brought down to earth when Lawrence and Frieda had sex in the olive groves.

They invested in wine, and hired a piano, brought round the coast in a rowing boat from La Spezia. Frieda sang and played German Folk Songs, in which the local Italians often joined.

She wrote to her sister: "This winter, I want to translate, and write and swim and fish and row. What else does one want?"

A year later, they had moved down to Florence and then Sicily, where Lawrence spent months finishing Lady Chatterley's Lover – the book with the engaging theme of an upper crust lady who found physical satisfaction in the clutches of a raw gamekeeper. How a highly intelligent wife could find life long fulfilment in such a preposterous embrace was one of the mysteries of Lawrence own emotions. Yet the book was banned until the 1960's by do-gooders and self regulators of a puritanical society.

Had Lawrence lived to a normal old age, he would have found himself a rich, revered figure, with film and literary rights. Instead the sallow, pallid, bearded Nottingham coal-miner's son looked back to England from sunnier climes, for a frank, fresh treatment of sex, whilst slowly dying of tuberculosis at the age of 44.

Neither Shelley nor Lawrence was keen swimmers. Shelley sank to the bottom of any water like a stone. Lawrence's lungs couldn't take the strain.

Lawrence remarked: "I don't swim more than a dozen yards, so am always trying to follow the starry Shelley".

"If you can't be a real poet," Frieda screamed at him across the water, "You'll die. Or at least you'll die like one."

'Death is the only pure conclusion of a great passion', he finally wrote.

We meandered further along to Tellaro. It had once been a well known smugglers den on a remote twisty track to a pirate's cove, almost at the end of the Peninsula.

"Ecco lo!" cried Angela, with her arms outstretched towards the Church.

It stood silhouetted in the murkiness on the rocky promontory. The bells tolled away mournfully, barely audible above the surging tide. It was almost as if they were calling the sailors to land before the Ponente stuck.

The three of us walked across the rocks to where the small fishing boats were again laid up for the coming winter, with their bottoms facing the sky. It was spell-binding Mediterranean magic. We finally reached the doors of the church on the rocks, perched high on the peninsula, proudly overhanging the water. The bell had stopped ringing, but from time to time the clock still struck out the late hours across the bay, facing defiantly towards the open Tirennian sea in the mournful gloom. Hemingway's "For Whom the Bell tolls" sprang to mind. We entered the church, dedicated to St. George. Inside, the crashing sound of the surf still echoed through the nave. It was almost as if a dragon, or a demon, was about to engulf us. In stormy winters, the priest's voice was barely audible. So wild and wicked were the waves, that one day – rumour has it - a giant squid grabbed the bell rope, which was trailing over the sea wall. The bells tolled to warn of invaders.

Facing due west, the last rays of the setting sun caught Napoleon's Corsica over the horizon.

In this bay of death, it was Love of Life that sprang to mind.

"Like Percy Shelley - to love two girls equally. For their mind, and their intellect, and their totally divergent idiosyncrasies; their whims, fads and fancies, passions and favours" volunteered Inge.

The three of us talked and walked, and laughed, and became too serious after drinking too much. We retraced our steps back to a restaurant at Lerici, set in a rock cave under the Norman Castle next to a tiny beach.

"Italy is so tender – like cooked macaroni – yards and yards of soft tenderness ravelled around everything" Lawrence had written.

Drowsy with good food and wine, well dined and wined, sleepy and content, our hearts and minds were on the same keel. We ended up together in the only bedroom available in the local tavern which greeted us at the end of that long line of shattering superlatives. This was earthquake territory. It really did move all three of us, as the bell tolled the hours away, from across those distant rocks.

I dozed off between them.

Gordon and Percy both loved this Bay, named after them - the Gulf of the Poets. They had between them the bond of the sea. From end to end, it is redolent of the redemptive healing power of the land of Italy and the seas that surround it.

I found myself alone, and then I realised why women make better romantics. My girlfriends deserted me to follow on later by bus. I went back around the furthest side of the Bay to reach Portovenere. The port was built by the Romans long before Christ, on the site of a temple to Venus.

It was from this thriving Portus Veneris that, in 1533, the ambitious 14 year old Florentine Catherine de Medici set sail for Marseille to marry Henry Duke of Orleans, who became King Henry II of France. Eccentric and ugly, she was a typical Medici. With a mouth too large and eyes too prominent to be a beauty, this ambitious teenager was to cause a revolution in France. A gastronomic one. Her motto was 'Hate and Wait'.

Container loads of delicious contraband were hoisted on board ship. She was taking with her tons of culinary implements and delicacies; along with a bevy of cooks, scullery maids, bottle washers and hangers on, as well as a retinue of the most talented chefs in Europe at that time. She was to sow the seeds of French culinary cuisine, based on the old Florentine principles

135

of simplicity, frugality and fresh local ingredients. For Florence - at the zenith of the Renaissance - was the culinary and cultural centre of Europe.

At that time French cuisine was a strange unappetising mix. It had strayed into an orgy of bacchanalian wastefulness and *nouveau riche* revelry. It was a heavy-handed dog's breakfast of shocking tastes. Fresh local produce was thrown out, and replaced by rich spicy luxuries and expensive, showy ingredients from far afild. Meals were so over prepared and over indulged as to be almost inedible. At orgies of gluttony and drunkenness, guests gorged themselves on salty, sauce-saturated, lurid ingredients. The highlight of a smart French dinner party was a parlour game, in which everyone was asked by the hostess to guess what food they had actually tasted.

Harmony and restraint, with simple unadulterated sauces, were what Catherine de Medici brought to French dinner tables. Her dishes complemented each other and stood on their own. Her chefs created onion soup, duck with orange sauce, guinea fowl with prunes, and wild boar with pine nuts.

Alongside the retinue of eager retainers that landed at Marseille was one reluctant man who was to revolutionise instant eating habits the world over. Alfredo Ruggieri was a simple Tuscan poultry farmer who cooked in his spare time. He had coolly asked permission to take part in one of Catherine's cooking competitions - normally only open to professional chefs. From hidden ingredients he produced a prize winning recipe. It was a small desert, which he had developed by trial and error, with the help of long forgotten recipe books. His little creation "flavoured water iced with sugar" was an instant success. The modern Sorbet Ice was born.

Ruggeri became the envy of others. He was bundled on board ship, protesting wildly, and ordered to produce his wonderful creation at Catherine's wedding banquet at Marseille. It turned out to be the flavour of the century. At banquet after banquet, he continued to produce exotic iced Sorbets, moulding them into elaborate shapes with numerous different flavours and colours. He became the envy of the culinary world. He was threatened, boycotted and beaten up by rival chefs in order to reveal his secret recipe. Frightened out of his wits, he eventually caved in. He wrote down the *modus operandi*, and sent it with a note to Catherine. "With your permission I wish to return to my chickens, hoping people will let me live in peace - and forget me". Catherine's chefs carried on the tradition of Tuscan Gelati.

Ice cream had been in Italy for 2000 years since the time of the Roman Emperor Nero, who ate 'sorbets' made with fruit, honey and snow. A thousand years later (in the late 9th century), Arabs brought it back to Italy when they invaded Sicily. In the 13th century Marco Polo returned from his travels to China with a recipe for sorbet, which for the first time included milk.

French table manners left a lot to be desired too. The far reaching Catherine brought the recently invented Italian table fork with her, and persuaded her son Henry to handle it with dexterity. However, she had no such luck with her sticky fingered and smelly old husband.

the French King, whose eating habits left little to the imagination.

Dinner parties were soon revolutionised. Heavy handed metal goblets were swapped for elegant Venetian glassware. Glazed earthenware was brought in from the workshops of Tuscany, to replace metal and wooden eating boards. Scrubbed tables were covered in fine linen table cloths and napkins.

Very soon, the old French Bacchanalian feasts became elegant Banquets - showcases of ceremony and fine wining and dining. Parisian hostesses soon vied with each other to produce the most sparkling results. Even Napoleons chef Antonin Careme, years later, declared that French chefs should first learn the arts of Catherine's Italian cooking and baking before they had a crack at their own French cuisine. This great hero-chef, who laid the foundations of French cuisine, had a tough upbringing. He was the 16th child of a stonemason, abandoned by his father at the age of 12 during the French revolution. Yet he finished up cooking for the Rothschilds.

It wasn't entirely a one way operation. Whilst the Trebbiano grape was brought into France from Italy; the Cabernet grape was smuggled back into Italy by Catherine's viticulturists and wine-makers - who envied the success of their French counterparts.

Overlooking the promontory of Portovenere at the end of the Peninsula, I wandered across to look down, far below, onto a cave at the sea's edge. The impetuous emerald and amethyst waves, streaked with white foam, crashed against the naked orange and grey rocks, and swept upwards over the smooth sloping entrance towards the cavern. Spread across this surface, higgledy-piggledy facing the sea lay a bevy of topless Italian girls, silently sporting tans all over. They were lazing languidly at Byron's Cove, where that "mad, bad and dangerous-to-know" poet had, by tradition, hung out. A nearby plaque enigmatically records the feats of this "immortal poet, who as a daring swimmer from Porto Venere to Lerici, defied the waves of the Ligurian Coast". Perhaps this was his one and only visit to his friend Percy Shelley who was enjoying his *ménage a trois* across the Bay.

A small group of sightseers stood watching. Down on the naked rocks, one of the bare breasted nymphs turned towards us, sauntering up the slippery slope, sure of herself, cockily tempting us from the dizzy distance.

I looked round, and beside me stood a pallid young man. He too was ogling the sinful sights beneath us, and was hobbling on an elegant walking stick. Perhaps in his thirties, he was sporting a flowing linen shirt, and baggy trousers with leather sandals. His bold appearance was accentuated by flowing chestnut curls across his brow, almost hidden by an ornate blue travelling cap which had been trimmed with gold braid. His moonlight pale visage was striking. He struck me immediately as the spit image of Gordon Byron. I turned to him. "I am Giles from Aberdeen; a Scottish crusader" he bragged, "born out of my time. Revolution is in my blood". He laughed. Then he came down to earth. "I come here every year. I am a Byron fan. I worked on the oil fields offshore from Aberdeen. Until

139

my accident. Byron was a strong swimmer; in spite of his lameness - his club foot. He never stopped bragging about swimming the Hellispont."

He pointed across the bay. "Can you imagine - all that way to visit Shelley, over there at Lerici. It's a marathon swim - four miles!"

We walked and talked, and sat down to muse at a portside café. Portovenere was bright and breezy, full of late summer trippers, and open to the whole Mediterranean western vista. I was entranced by the knowledge of this pilgrim, following in the footsteps of that very mortal wordsmith:

"Like him, I went to Aberdeen Grammar School. They've got a bust of him there. He had a good education but a miserable time. A gloomy old Calvinistic upbringing. His uncouth mother dominated him. She harped on his lameness and warped his character. Drove him to pessimism. He never loved her. She was a typical product of the wild Gordon clan. Two of her relatives killed themselves.

"His father's side wasn't much better either. Totally debauched. The only good thing they did was to marry into money. Then a great uncle blew it. He flogged off half the family estates, massacred all the stags and deer, cut down the centuries old oak trees, flogged off the family silver, and went into terminal decline. Gordon took over at the age of 10.

"Of course, in his 20's he had his passions. Even then, women were more liberated than they thought. An extrovert like Byron took advantage, and it worked magic. The mermaid on his family crest was a fatal omen. He knew he was going to die young. And he relished every moment of it – especially here in Italy."

"Shall we go for swim? At Byron's Cove," I suggested.

"Since my accident I can't swim" he responded coldly.

"Just like Percy Shelley" I muttered "The sea can be a fatal attraction."

"Just like mermaids on the rocks," he added.

So we sat on the seafront, and gorged ourselves on the simplest dish around. Sardines - from the Latin word Sarda - are named from their home territory across these waters – Sardinia. They are still caught off shore by the fishermen, who range far out to sea, avoiding the Ponente and Levant winds, to mine this delicious and declining 'silver from the sea'.

'A woman and a sardine are both finer when most petite', goes an old Sardinian proverb. It was almost as if that bloody-minded independent Island has an age-old vendetta against mainland Tuscany

"Yes, the smallest ones are best," said the restaurateur, "and the best time to eat them is Spring and Summer - between June and October."

We gorged ourselves on them – gutted and filled simply with a breaded mixture of milk, eggs, parmesan, marjoram, garlic, then sprinkled with olive oil and breadcrumbs. The Sardinian 'vendetta' appeared in the mildest form - a dash of hot chili. So fresh was the fish that they needed little more than a quick searing over the open charcoals to be grilled to crispy perfection. I helped myself to a clean fork from the adjoining table. Italy's great invention is still

141

seemingly so prestigious that only one fork per person is allowed - in normal circumstances.

We quaffed the local wine with a whiff of the sea, from the Apuan hills above Massa; the same wine that Napoleon's soldiers had waxed lyrical about.

There are four seas around Italy. The Ligurian, the Tyrrhenian, the Ionian and the Adriatic. The Mediterranean Sea only flows south of Sicily.

As we looked out from that harbour on the Ligurian coast, a shimmering modern maritime image steeled across the horizon - from who knows where. In the hazy distance, a dazzling white yacht emerged. It did not touch shore, but took a long, languid breather, in full view of us landlubbers, simmering and brooding in the 'heat of history'. It then slowly turned northwards to disappear again over the horizon towards France.

As we sat there in that late summer of 1997, it was the ill-fated voyage carrying Diana and Dodi, after they had visited Corsica, on their way back to the Riviera – taking them back to their tragic demise in the Paris tunnel.

**"Noon descends and after noon,**
**Autumn's evening meets me soon -**
**Leading the infantine moon".**

Shelley:    Lines written
amongst the Euganean Hills.

# Chapter 8

## THE MARBLE COAST

Beyond the nasty naval sprawl of La Spezia, the lusty old Magra River still holds its own, running noisily into the sea. One side of the river is in Liguria; the other side heralds the sandy shores of Tuscany, and the greatest marble quarries in the world, centred on the cities of Massa and Carrara.

The Magra was always a decadent old waterway, overlooked by the ancient Roman citadel of Luni, which dominated the mouth of the river. So magnificent and spectacular were the town's ancient walls, marble monuments and decorated mansions, that when the Viking King Hastings rampaged down here in the 9th century, he thought he had reached Rome, and had conquered the whole world.

Long before the Romans arrived, scattered marble deposits were found around this stretch of coastline by the ancient Etrsucans. They carved small artefacts, and decorated their houses with it.

After the demise of the Etruscans, the Liguri settled here. They were ardent fighters against the Romans, and held out longer and braver than most. Whilst the Romans used the deep-water port for their ambitious conquest of the Spanish, the Liguri continued their resistance to Roman occupation. So with the help of Danish mercenaries, the Romans deported tens of thousands of men, women and children *en masse* to Naples. Then they developed the city. Luni became a thriving town, producing the best wine in the region, and cheese from the local black sheep, still grazing benignly around the local pastures. When the Magra River silted up, Luni was left stranded a mile inland.

It gave its name to the adjacent mountainous region of Lunigiana. Not an arid moonscape, it is dominated by the distant Apennine peaks, clouded with pine and chestnut forests. Nearer to the coast are the Apuan Alps - all flaked in marble dust, snowy white in the glaring sunshine.

When the Emperor Augustus nationalised most of the quarries throughout the Roman Empire, Luni's privately owned quarries were left alone.

Roman sculptors relied less and less on imported pure white Greek marble. They soon found the white marble of Punta Bianca*, the nearby promontory jutting out to sea, before they stumbled upon the Carrara variety with its own unique luminescence and fine structure.

In the 15th century Carrara fell under the Blackthorns – descendants of the Cybo Malaspina family. It then became part of the Duke of Modena's territory, until it finally joined the Republic of Genoa.

Corsica, the Balearic Islands, Monte Carlo and Nice all came under the control of the immensely wealthy maritime Republic of Genoa.

---

*Protecting the harbour of La Spezia, the strategically placed Punta Bianca is where the Germans trained their massive guns out to sea against an expected WWII marine invasion which never materialised.*

Thriving Nice - Nizza in Italian - was the Republic's uneasy frontier county with France. It was tossed between its three neighbours – France, the Republic of Genoa and the Kingdom of Savoy.

There was an uneasy truce. From day to day, no one could decide which way the wind was blowing. Neither this way, nor that. "Ni Zi! Ni Za!" they declared; and so the name *Nizza* stuck. Its own dialect and national anthem 'Nissa La Bella' remain today.

The County of Nice was finally ceded to France in 1860 as a reward for helping to drive the Austrians out of Italy. Giuseppe Garibaldi, born in Nice, strongly opposed this hand-over, and strove for a return of the County to a united Italy.

The Republic of Genoa's seafaring superstars, Marco Polo, Christopher Columbus and Andrea Doria, all roamed its ports as boys.

The last of Genoa's Imperial sons was Napoleon Bonaparte. The residence of the Buonaparte family - originally from Pisa - became Sarzana, until they finally moved out to the island of Corsica. Napoleon was born in Corsica only a few months after it was reluctantly rented out to France by the Republic of Genoa. After 400 years they had been unable to tame the Corsican bandits. The option to revert back to Genoa was never taken up. So Napoleon naturally became a *'Frog'* by force of circumstances. His home language was Corsican Italian – a cross between the Genoese and Tuscan dialects. His French was far from perfect. In fact he was little more French in language and habits than any other Italian living in France. He remained very much a Corsican bandit to the end.

Napoleons elderly mother outlived all her family. Madame Mere (nee Letizia Ramolino), spent her declining years in Rome. After the fall of the French Empire she returned more than once to visit her Italian roots, including the tiny village of Aiaccio between Pisa and Livorno, as she passed along the Aurelian way to and from Paris.

We continued our rumble along the line to Carrara. One look up to the hills behind proclaims the city's fame for its white inheritance, which through the centuries was fought over by almost everyone in sight. Colossal 10 square metre blocks are hewn from the mountain pinnacles, and slid down time-worn torturous routes, once by oxen and man-power, now by 20 wheel drive vehicles.

**'And the rocks above and the streams below, and the Apennines shroud of summer snow'.**

Even Percy Shelley was taken in by it all.

Local legend has a twist. Carrara's God given wealth was really the result of a mistake by a lazy angel. When God was creating the world, he grew weary. So he asked two angels to make the finishing touches to the Italian peninsula, by forming the mountains with loads of various rocks, granite and marble. One angel was industrious, and flew off to the north, where he deposited his various loads in different spots to make the Alps. The other angel flew south. On the way he stopped for a siesta on the beach below Carrara. Waking up in a panic, he realised his mistake and dumped all his loads of marble in one spot, creating the mountains above Carrara. Back in heaven, God was very angry, but instead of punishing the angel, he relented. "Never mind," he declared: "Now you have made the marble mountains, artists will come from all over the world and make beautiful sculptures." [1]

Many of Carrara's streets and pavements are covered with the bright white - and sometimes not so white - marble. The river is filled with small chippings - some collector's items, many covered in moss or lichen. Precious few still retain time-worn elements of a once unfinished masterpiece.

Fought over by Lucca, Florence and Milan, it was a struggle between the good the bad and the down right ugly. The medieval bishop counts of Luni and the landed aristocracy started the ball rolling. Then the Guilds and Unions of the local families vied with each other.

**Carrara – dead are the bishops and counts of Luni, and their tombs are dispersed . . .**
**But instead, over these cities reign fair heroes**
**Born in the womb of your mountains.**

The prodigious Poet, Playwright, Author and 'Father of Fascism', Gabriele D'Annunzio gave an optimistic classical slant to the modern heirs of this feudal clan, which through the centuries jealously controlled their quarries.

This romantic soldier, flyer, mariner and revolutionary – who became a legend in his own lifetime and a model for radical leaders all over the world - went to school in Tuscany, and lived for a while on the coast at Viareggio.

147

After the First World War D'Annunzio campaigned widely for Italy to side with the Allies and become a first ranking European power, with an African Empire. When the isthmus port city of Fiume on the Adriatic coast (now Rijeka in Croatia) which had a majority Italian population, was handed over at the Paris Peace Conference, D'Annunzio led his 'legions' to seize it back. His private army of 2000 irregular troops, aided by a mutinous Italian Navy destroyer, forced out the American, British and French occupying forces. With wide ranging support from the outlying Italian Diaspora, he declared war on Italy, and planned a march on Rome. He only surrendered a year later when Fiume was bombarded by the Italian Navy.

During his occupation of Fiume he formulated the ideals and rituals of Fascism, which were followed by Mussolini. These included the dramatic balcony harangues, the Roman salute, the use of religious symbols and attendant black shirted followers - along with some of their more sordid strong-arm tactics. With the leader of the mutinous seamen De Ambris, he co-authored a Constitution. This included nine corporations covering the different sectors of the economy, and a tenth – added by D'Annunzio – to represent the 'superior' human beings such as heroes, poets and prophets. Music was also a fundamental principle of the state.

He retired to his sumptuous villa on Lake Garda, and became utterly disillusioned with Mussolini's idea of fascism, and his alliance with Hitler, which he tried hard to break. He died in 1938, a year before the outbreak of World War II.

Carrara is a city of song and stone. The beautiful opera house has miraculous acoustics. The stonemason's themselves disgorge *Bel Canto* in their own unmusical, guttural and almost unintelligible dialect called 'Carrarino'. With its clipped endings, hard consonants, slight nasality and pinging, percussive rhythms, it almost sounds like chisels tapping against stone.[1]

The otherwise inauspicious surroundings do not attract the hordes of trippers who dash in and out of the *centro storico* on marble pilgrimages. They stay in the beachside hotels down the road. It hasn't changed for generations.

When Dickens called here in the 1850s he described Carrara as "very harsh and picturesque, where few tourists stayed." He marvelled at the "exquisite marble shapes that grew out of all this toil and sweat and torture." He concluded: "Every good thing has its birth in sorrow and distress".

The railroad became strategic to Carrara's wealth, for shipping by sea had been the only way out of this torturous territory. From the 1850's onwards it prospered on the movement of the immense tonnage of marble of all shapes, sizes and hues, to the cities of the newly unified nation.

Dickens recorded how the then Duke of Modena, who owned this territory was an odd wag.

"He was also much opposed to railroads. If certain lines planned by other potentates on either side of him had been executed, he would have probably enjoyed the satisfaction of having an omnibus plying to and fro across his not very vast dominions, to forward travellers from one terminus to another." [2]

Late in the railway game, Italy quickly caught up. In 1850 the first line from Rome to Frascati had been built – almost as a novelty. In contrast to the Duke of Modena, the old railway enthusiast Pio Nono (Pope Pius IX) had given his whole-hearted blessing to this new fangled invention, which would eventually reach up to Tuscany and beyond. It would be a heaven sent opportunity to join his Papal States with most of Italy's coastal cities on the western seaboard, from Genoa to Naples. At the opening ceremony a cavalcade of red robed Cardinals sang its praises.

In Rome itself, the Pope watched with quiet fascination the erection of a new steel bridge across the Tiber - designed and constructed by the British Contractor John Oliver North. On this auspicious occasion, the Pope was greeted by a polite Englishman, who introduced himself as the British Minister of Public Works. He had been reluctant to be seen by the Pontiff as he was carrying an umbrella and work clothes - a grey coat and a straw hat. The Pope informed him that his attire was of no importance since he had been taken unawares, and added: "Now you can say in London that the Roman Pontiff is not always at prayer surrounded by incense, monks and priests. Tell the Queen that Her Majesty's Minister of Public Works found the old Pope surrounded by his engineers whilst helping to finish a new railway bridge across the Tiber.[3]

And then, for half an hour, we bussed up to the marble quarry village of Colonnata. Named after a colony of slaves, it lies where the strongest and most durable marble is found. It was used by the ancient

Romans for their heaviest structural projects and weight bearing arches.

Five hundred metres above sea level, Colonnata is one of the highest of the 'marble' villages - and home to the hardiest quarry men who climb the mountains and rip out the blocks by brute force. It is the only village where the marble workers walk down-hill to work.

As their skills have been handed down, so too has their culinary expertise. The gastronomic Romans started the trend. Experts at meat curing, they perfected the art of squeezing slabs of pig fat between marble slabs to produce high energy food. Local herbs and sea water flavoured this delicacy.

Here the best Lardo di Colonnata is formed, or rather squeezed and pressed for months on end - between blocks of the finest close grained Carrara marble - six inches thick.

Only the purest slabs, with no porosity, are good enough. This keeps the temperature constant. And only the best local Tuscan swine pork fat is used. It comes from the *Cintra Sinese* pigs, nurtured on the prolific chestnuts from the local woods, wafted by sea breezes to give a delicate melt-in-the-mouth texture to the lard. Each local family guards its own secret recipe. The pig fat is pressed with herbs and spices, sometimes aided by garlic and peppercorns, cinnamon, oregano, basil, fennel, nutmeg, rosemary, mint and even dried carnations.

Delicate shades of pink, gold and off-white perfect the taste, but the pure lardo from these parts contains not a trace of bacon meat, which would ruin the flavour. The finished block is sliced paper thin. It is spread on *crostini*, and toasted quickly to bring out the flavour; used in pizzas, or eaten raw.

There are plenty of copiers around, but the best Lardo still comes from Colonnata. It has been awarded European wide Protected Geographical status, just like Champagne.

Right on the main line is the station of Pietra Santa, the prosperous city of smart sculptors, including Henry Moore. Once a separate enclave in the Republic of Lucca it lies strategically on the old Roman Aurelian way. Its name derives not from the 'Holy Stone', but from its origin in 1215 when the Republic of Lucca ordered a local nobleman called Pietrasanta to develop a town on the strategic route between mountains and sea. Its situation in the foothills was forced upon the ancient inhabitants by the malaria swamps of the coastal plain. Only modern drainage methods brought respite, and created new seaside resorts like Forte dei Marmi.

We arrived at 'The Fort of Marble' and spread ourselves through the gardens along the sea front. From this very spot in 1520, Michelangelo's best marble was brought down from the hills above. Before a new wharf was constructed, oxen and muscle-men would drag the stone blocks to the sandy shores, and then float the waiting boats up onto the beach. The blocks would be manhandled up earthen ramps, over log rollers, or hoisted with rope winches slung over the boats; then eased over the bulwarks onto the ships decks. The boats would then wait for the rising tide to float them out to sea. They were shipped down the coast for

Michelangelo's masterpieces in Florence and Rome. In unguarded moments, many of the huge pieces were stolen from the seashore by rival sculptors.

Towering over us, more than 1500 metres high, and only 7 miles as the gulls fly from the coast, was Monte Altissimo. On its marble peak Michelangelo once planned a gigantic sculpture to be viewed from miles out to sea.

With an air of relaxed sophistication we sat for lunch at one of the hundreds of restaurants which litter the beach road as far as the eye can see. The old pine forests have all but disappeared, so there are very few breathing spaces anywhere along this coast line. Once in a while there is a break - a drab undeveloped stretch, with no raked sand, which heralds a *Spiaggia Libera* - a Free Beach.

A few speed boats break the silence - trailing skiers in white foam. Waiters wend their way between the endless rows of sun beds lined up in military precision. Milanese Captains of Industry and Russian Oligarchs sprawl like alley-cat emperors on huge, dazzling beach beds, whilst eyeing Armani and Valentino bikinis. Beach bimbos outnumber the locals two to one. On wilder nights, at late-night bars, hippie hardcore chicks, who find it harder to get into their clothes than out of them, boogie on bar tops, showering in Prosecco.

Bicycles are the preferred means of transport here, and small private villas with gardens, fountains and pools are the smartest hotels of all for the *Giro Giusto* – the right circle. This was the favourite beachside resort of the Ciano family before the War.

Count Ciano was Mussolini's son in law. He was shot on the orders of Il Duce.

Mussolini also had a good bash at banning spaghetti and macaroni from the national diet. It wasn't just a war-time economy measure. The whole idea was to drag the munching proletariat into modern *culinaria*. But try as he may, he was outwitted. There was so much opposition, including protests from expatriate Italians in America, that he was forced to retreat. Yet all the while, he had clean forgotten about the *Mangia Fagioli* - the hardy Bean Eaters of Tuscany, who thrived and survived.

"It is especially the Inglese, who think of Pasta as a meal in itself – an alternative to Pizza," the local restaurateur instructed us.

As we drank the local Tuscan Rose from goldfish bowl glasses he droned on in the heat::

"It is very flattering for us. Once the basic food, pasta is now in smartest Italian circles, the first course – consumed after canapés, and before the main course."

"*Salto il Primo*" I cry, "I'll skip the first course."

"I'd like the sea bass with shallots" declared Inge.

I order a Bistecca Fiorentina, a giant T bone, with the meat on both sides of the bone - the fillet and the sirloin. "Beefsteak from the Cow" I explain. Not a Bistecca Maile – a Pork Chop. Nor a Bistecca they serve in parts of France which comes from Horsemeat.

---

[1] Quoted in **Michelangelo's Mountain** by Eric Scigliano
[2] Charles Dickens : **Pictures of Italy.**
[3] P.M. Kalla-Bishop. **Italian Railroads.**
As told in **Blood Iron & Gold** by Christian Wolmar

# Chapter 9

# WAR IN THE APUAN ALPS

The narrow strip of Tuscan coastal land between the sea and the mountains which now includes the Autostrada and the main Railway line was of savage, strategic importance to the retreating Germans in 1944. They had been chased all the way up Italy by the Americans and the Brits under General Alexander.

Nothing worried this charming Irish gentleman. Throughout history, the Paddies produced superb Generals. Wellington, Wolseley, Kitchener, French, Alanbrooke, Alexander and Montgomery were all Irish.

When France collapsed at the beginning of the War, Alexander was the last man to leave Dunkirk. Montgomery later became his deputy - after he had cleaned the enemy out of North Africa.

In Italy however, after landing in the island of Sicily, the dilatory Montgomery took a leisurely 'promenade' up the coast to Messina, facing the Italian mainland only 10 miles across the straights of Messina. The American General Clark was meanwhile struggling up through the mountainous centre of the island, also hoping to win the race to Italy's toe. Montgomery loathed Americans in general - and Clark in particular - and was itching to be called to the rescue of his hard pressed American colleague. Everything came to a head at the Salerno landings in the Gulf of Naples. While the two Allied commanders were indulging in point scoring, the Germans missed their opportunity on the beachhead. When they finally pulled back, north of Naples, they formed the Gustav Line across Italy.

Having finally crashed through the Gustav and Caesar Lines, it was General Alexander who drove the Germans up and out of Rome. For this he was made a Field Marshall. He met his match with Field Marshall Kesselring. There was a sort of school boyish rake about both of them. Kesselring was called 'Smiling Albert' for his toothy grin and cheeky face. He was a military genius with unquenchable optimism. He harried the Allies advance up to the Alps for nearly 2 years (608 days). And although he revelled in 'Bavarian bonhomie' he harboured streaks of barbarity.

On their retreat through Tuscany the Germans finally formed the Gothic Line. Defended by over two thousand fortified machine gun posts, this formidable barrier ran for 200 miles from the coast between Viareggio and La Spezia, through the foothills of the Apennines, across to the Adriatic Sea at Rimini.

The Gothic Line was to be the final stand of the Germans, when all else had failed. It was a long and bitter struggle. All hell broke loose. The refugees swarmed out from the coastal cities. The partisans retreated to the mountains, hiding in huts and caves.

Alexander exhorted the Italian partisans to harass the retreating Germans at every opportunity on the Gothic Line. In response, Kesselring personally ordered reprisals of 10 civilians for every German soldier killed. Atrocities became commonplace.

On the western side, the partisans grouped in scattered bunches such as the Garibaldi Brigade, with smaller groups such as Ugo Muccini, Guido Boscagliago, and Gino Lombardi forming the nucleus. Holed up in the mountains of Versilia and Garfagnana - nearly two thousand metres high - were the Group of Apuan Patriots. They reached down to sabotage and frustrate the Nazi-Fascist enemy. Meanwhile the Americans were lumbering around - strafing and taking out beautiful mediaeval bridges from the air, and sometimes shooting up innocent civilian convoys.

We arrived at the nearly deserted hamlet of Sant' Anna di Stazzema. It was the scene of one of the most cowardly mass murders in war torn Italy.

Since the days of the Grand Duchy of Tuscany this peaceful pastoral mountain hamlet, a few miles inland from Pietrasanta and north-west of Camaiore had lived a simple life based on charcoal and chestnuts.

**"Little groups of houses dotted here and there**
**under the pathways of the peaks . . .**
**Under the protection of St Anne"**

In August 1944, in the impending confrontation against the partisans and advancing Allied forces, the area around Stazzema had been specially earmarked for total evacuation of all civilians. A delegation of local Parish Priests went to the Germans to protest. They warned: 'Beware! These mountain folk are proud and tenacious people who will not be easily budged or pushed around'. To no avail. The order stood. [1]

Moreover, the Group of Apuan Patriots baited the Germans, ordering them to evacuate the area themselves. Posters were printed urging people to disobey the German orders, and stay put. This sealed the fate of the inhabitants of Sant' Anna.

The whole village was razed to the ground in murderous reprisal. 560 people were rounded up by the diabolically efficient Nazi-Fascists. They were shot and incinerated. The young men had escaped into the mountains thinking their families would be safe. The parish priest had rung the bells to warn of danger. "The enemy are coming. Retreat! Hide in the mountains," the church bells tolled. An SS reconnaissance unit arrived - guided by local fascists. They found the entire village empty except for women, children and the old folk huddled mainly in and around the Church. They shot the priest at point blank. The rest were rounded up and gunned down. Their bodies were disposed of by burning the Church pews. Others who had hidden in the cellars were incinerated when grenades were thrown in. The church organ was blown to pieces by the Germans, thinking it was a hiding place.

From the restored church square, we struggled up the Way of the Cross. It's a long, symbolic climb. Every few hundred metres, along the deliberately sharp stony pathway, is embedded one of a dozen bas-relief images, linking the massacre with the sufferings of Christ on the Via Dolorosa to Calvary.

In the woods at the summit, stands a huge stone Memorial, containing the bones of the 560 victims it was possible to identify, with their names inscribed nearby. From the chestnut and cedar groves, that once brought prosperity to this pastoral hamlet, the Ossuary looks down to the coast, two thousand feet below. Overall, pervades a distinct air – not of tragedy – but of strange Tuscan tranquillity. Not even the birds sing. For

Peace is what this Park is all about - in memory of all wars; at all times; everywhere.

Down in the Museum of Resistance we catch the most poignant image of all. It is a faded black and white photograph of a group of 20 children, dancing round the school playground, holding hands, singing ring-a-ring of roses - Italian style. Few survived.

As a young man, Elio Toaff, who hailed from La Spezia, had scrambled up to these mountains from Livorno, along with numerous other refugees from the coastal cities. His dark looks, aquiline nose and haunting eyes spoke of local origins. Yet he was Jewish, and was later to become a Chief Rabbi of Rome. Like many ordinary Italians he had escaped into the hills, surviving on bread from chestnut flour and any other food that was available. The day before the massacre, he was captured with a group of Partisans by the SS. They assumed he was one of them. He was marched off to a wooded clearing, and saw his comrades hanged from the trees. "For me, all that was left was to pray" he recalled. Not so, however. He attracted the attention of the Officer in command of the SS - an Austrian Captain. "Tell me, do you have a family?" he asked. "Yes, a wife and baby," I replied. The Officer spoke: "I too have a wife and child back in Vienna. I am Professor of Mathematics at the University there." To my surprise, the captain ordered: 'Take this one outside'.

"I was marched out, and found myself alone with the Captain. He fired a shot in the air, and I escaped down the mountain.

"A while later, I returned to St Anna with my

companions, after having heard of the carnage there. In a stable there was a pile of corpses - 80 or perhaps 100. They were deformed, unrecognisable, still burning. After having locked the people inside the building, the SS had set fire to the straw, throwing in hand grenades, setting fire to those still alive.

"I went into a house. The door was open. I saw a woman seated on a chair. I went to speak to her. The dead woman had an open womb. The baby, just born, and already slaughtered by the SS, was lying on a table with its umbilical chord still attached to the mother. The Nazis had shot them in the temple with a pistol. That image has haunted my dreams for years." [2]

For 50 years, evidence of the massacre was hidden in archives. In 1994, it was revealed that a metal filing cabinet had been turned back against the wall; its drawers jammed shut, in a basement of a Rome prosecutor's office. When it was finally opened, it was packed full of yellowing files full of shameful secrets.

The truth is that the men who led the Germans were local fascists. Thinly disguised, they spoke in unmistakeable accents, using words, phrases and local dialect. This, perhaps, would explain why the truth was hidden - rather the post war process of reconciliation.

Kesselring himself had blood on his hands. Yet after the war he was spared the death sentence, mainly on the recommendation of Churchill and Alexander.

60 years on, in 2004, an aged German soldier turned up and confessed he was so ashamed of what he had done at Sant' Anna that he had suffered nightmares ever since. Unable to reconcile his shameful deeds, he had travelled from Germany to repent his crime, at the

recently reopened War Crimes Tribunal at La Spezia. His case was reverently rushed through. Not as a case of tit for tat, but as a process of reconciliation, to lay the spectre to rest. Yet none of the others involved, either living in retirement in Germany, or the local Fascists, came forward to testify. Many of them were tried *in absentia*, and sentenced to life imprisonment.

Major Walter Reder, in command of another SS unit, was a man well known for similar atrocities on the Gothic Line. He was one of the few Germans to be finally brought to trial for the massacre of Marzabotto – one of the worst in Europe - in the mountains south of Bologna, in which 772 civilians were killed.

Of the estimated total number of victims, 45 were less than 2 years old, 110 were less than 10 years old, 95 were less than 16 years old, 142 were more than 60 years old, 316 were women, and 5 were Catholic priests.

I had an uneasy feeling all around this fertile area of the Gothic Line. I recalled a little pilgrimage we had made on the other side of the mountain to a favourite restaurant in that region. It stands like a neat Swiss chalet, overlooking the Serchio River. .

We had lunched for next to nothing on the lovely local food with wine. Afterwards we wandered up to Monte Perpoli, high above the Serchio Valley. Outside the remote church, all was uncannily quiet. A lonesome image stared at us in poignant reminder. It was a small plaque set into the wall. A faded photograph in a watertight frame held the face of a local Italian - not a youth; not a partisan. He was a man pushing 40. To strangers, like me, lost in the mists of time, he had died simply: A Prisoner in Germany 1944.

Like so many others who had been captured, or had changed sides, or had surrendered to the Allies when the tide had turned, he was rounded up by the remaining Nazi-Fascists and sent to Germany for forced labour. More than 40,000 former Italian soldiers died in prison camps. I wondered who had turned tale.

Hereabouts, there was also a feeling of *deja vue*. Was it not in Parma lying just across the mountains, that in 1806 Napoleon, the cruel little Corsican whose family had originally hailed from Pisa, had ordered his French security chief to put down an insurrection by almost identical draconian means. "Burn 5 or 6 villages, shoot the priest and 60 people, send three or four hundred to the galleys!" he had ordered his extremely reluctant General Junot. "We do not share the same idea of clemency. I do not share your opinion as to the innocence of Parmese peasants!" [3]

We met one of the larger than life Tuscans from Pietrasanta who travelled the world and sometimes returns to her roots. She was raised on the edge of the Apuan Alps, where the wealth of many families came from the centuries old marble quarries.

Her mother was in a Group of partisan patriots. The Germans were after her. "I was sent to stay with my aunt. My name was changed, whilst my mother launched into partisan business in the mountains. They went to attack a German outpost, and she told the others in her group, "When I throw a hand grenade 'DUCK'. She threw the grenade. It missed its target, and an innocent old lady nearby was killed by mistake."

Her mother always reckoned her parish priest was unforgiving for this unfounded killing, even though such acts of violence by the partisans could, and did, bring on even worse reprisals. Many parish priests had been shot or hanged by the Germans for trying to intercede in the civil war between right and left.

So, she concluded: "The Pope was pro Nazi."

Far from it. Pope Pius XII was one of the leading pro-Jewish politicians of his day. The Vatican saved more Jews from the Holocaust than all the Allied Powers put together. Between 700,000 to 800,000 to be exact. America, due to its rigid quota system, accepted less than 20,000 Jewish refugees during the entire War. Britain took only about 80,000.

Pope Pius ordered all the convents and monasteries in Rome to be used as safe havens, and handed over all the gold he could muster to the diabolical SS Chief. He also persuaded the Military Chief of Rome - an Austrian General of the old school - to desist from hounding out and deporting Jews. This was achieved on the pretext of being too time consuming, and wasteful of military man power.

In Holland, the Dutch Bishops had already strongly denounced the Nazis from the Catholic pulpits. As a result, all the remaining Jews in Holland were rounded up and sent to concentration camps, including those who had converted to Christianity. Pope Pius considered a stronger and wider response to this outrage. His Bavarian housekeeper, Mother Pasqualina, recalled how he reluctantly changed his mind. As she watched him burning the notes of his denunciation with his own hands in the Vatican kitchens, he commented

"What would my denunciation, which is stronger than theirs, achieve? Perhaps even worse reprisals."

The Chief Rabbi of Rome was so impressed with the work of the Vatican, that after the War he became a Catholic and changed his name to Pius.

The dignified old British Minister to the Holy See, Sir D'Arcy Osborne, who spent most of the war holed up in the Vatican, considered Pius to be the most saintly person he had ever encountered in his long life.

Most evenings, away from the bowing and saluting of St Peters, Sir D'Arcy would take a relaxing stroll to exercise his aged cairn terrier in the Vatican gardens. He often met his friend Harold Tittmann, the American Chargé d'Affairs, who also had a pet dog. Their favourite resting place was a little renaissance pavilion, where they sat together, gazing at the giant radiance of Michelangelo's dome set against the backdrop of the Vatican's power station and radio masts. They were not even on nodding terms with the pro-Petain French Ambassador, so their eyes were averted when his clumsy Gallic sheepdog snuffled by, and took an aversion to their Anglo American pets.

Time glosses over the inevitable. Many modern Italian historians maintain that Italian fascists were fighting for their country just as much as anti fascists were: "Atrocities were committed on both sides."

Florence brought out the best and the worst. Throughout the War two British teenagers risked their lives daily working as couriers for British Intelligence, and to help Allied airmen escape. Giovanna and her sister Pauline were brought up in India. Their father was an Italian diplomat, their mother an English lady of the tea estates variety. Thus they had no particular attachment to any country. They were in due course sent to Italy with the Nuns at the international school in Florence. When Italy joined the War in 1940 Giovanna was 19 and her sister 17; poised to go to University. Many of the Professors were Jewish. They disappeared and were never seen again. Working in British territory, their Italian father was unable to get back to Italy. He was taken in by the British, and sent to the Eldoret Internment Camp in East Africa. Their mother, having an Italian passport as well as a British one, managed to avoid been taken prisoner, even though she was known as the '*Inglese.*' With two daughters, it was a struggle.

The countryside was dotted with groups of partisans and escaped British prisoners of war holed up in the woods. They were secretly supported by a network which inevitably included the girls and their English mother. Discovery by the Germans – or betrayal by local fascists – would have sent her to a concentration camp. A kindly Swiss couple living in Florence one day approached their mother. Would she mind if their daughter Giovanna went with them up into the mountains. She was fluent in French and English as well as Italian. It was to meet groups of escaped prisoners of war and downed airmen, and plan an operation to help them escape into Switzerland or across the border into southern France and then Spain. This she dutifully did. Their removal to a network of safe houses became a regular occurrence.

"We were only allowed to contact one person, and to speak to no one else, except my mother."

Her next task was to work as a Red Cross nurse

in the hospital in Florence. The Doctor in charge never divulged that she was British.

"One day we were warned to expect a group of British prisoners in the hospital for treatment. When they turned up they were nearly all Generals, or of a very senior rank, including General Carton de Wiart - the one with the patch over his eye, who had been captured in Libya. The liaison officer was Brigadier the Earl of Ranfurley. It was him I fell for. So I became the go between, and received regular notes to hide in my bilious uniform to smuggle out to my Swiss contacts."

The Generals were all prisoners incarcerated in a marvellous old mediaeval villa – Castello di Vincigliata at Fiesole outside Florence.

"They soon started digging a tunnel, which was launched from the other end by some Italian partisans".

In all, Carton de Wiart made five attempts to escape. Once he evaded capture for 8 days disguised as an Italian peasant; no mean feat considering he was in Italy, did not speak Italian and was 61 years old with an eye patch, one empty sleeve and multiple injuries.

"Unfortunately there was a turncoat - an Italian fascist who reported me. I was taken in and questioned, but managed to get away. I disappeared across the hills near Siena. Not so my sister, who was 17 at the time. She was picked up and questioned. 'Where is your sister!' they asked. 'I don't know' she replied, 'and even if I did I would not tell.'

"She was imprisoned for 6 months in solitary confinement. She told them nothing. Eventually they threw her out. They needed the cell for another prisoner. Again she went back to prison in a group cell with many of the local Italian aristocrats - the de Medici included. The war was nearing an end so they let her out. As the British advanced up the eastern flank, I met my husband." [4]

General Carton de Wiart had in fact been approved for repatriation due to his disablement. In 1943 he was taken from his prison and driven to Rome. Italy was trying to get out of the war, and backdoor negotiations were going slowly. He was instructed to accompany an Italian negotiator General Zanussi to Lisbon to meet Allied contacts to facilitate surrender.

The Germans sent into Florence teams of constructors and carpenters to board up important old buildings and treasure troves. Some areas and buildings were strictly out of bounds except to the officials. Reality came with the liberation.

As the Allies advanced north, driving the enemy before them, the German looted and plundered from Museums whenever and wherever they could. On arrival at Florence, which had been declared an Open City, the Allies approached the most sacred of bridges - the Ponte Vecchio – the only one left standing. The partisans were on the far bank. There was no way across, and no way out. The ancient secret passageway, once used by the Medicis, linking the Pitti Palace with the Uffizi across the bridge, had been compromised. So under the noses of the German guards, they ran a telephone line under the arches, tied to the bulwarks. Messages confirmed highly unusual activity for Museums and Art Galleries. Specialists and experts were alerted. When Allied troops finally advanced they discovered the first depots to which treasures of the

Pitti, the Uffizi and other Galleries had been removed.

As the Germans retreated further north, the treasures went with them. Many known deposits were found empty, and the Allies heard from local eyewitnesses that German troops had moved the entire contents as the battle line approached.

Almost at the very end of the war, there was a remarkable find on the borders of Austria, above Bolzano, in the German speaking part of Italy. This was an area only nominally Italian, since the Third Reich had already earmarked it for 'easy takeover'. Two huge storage depots were discovered by the advancing Allies, containing priceless art treasures. One was in the Val Passiria area above Merano, and the other at Campo Tures in the Valle Aurina above Brunico.[5]

Captured members of the German Fine Arts Unit at Bolzano admitted a strange tale of honest duplicity, allied with opportunism, for the enrichment of the Third Reich at the expense of Italy. In fact, the Fascists had already prepared perfectly safe storage facilities in the Lakes area of Italy. They were never used. Even Mussolini himself had protested, to no avail, at the removal of Italy's greatest treasures to within 30 kilometres of the Austrian frontier.

Had the War gone the other way, there is not the slightest doubt that they would have ended up being part of the Reich.

[1]  Quoted in **Italy's Sorrow** – James Holland
[2] Interview of Elio Toaff with **Gente** Magazine 2003.
[3]  St Cloud Archives. Quoted in **Napoleon** by Robert Asprey.
[4] Interview of Giovanna Ellis with Author
[5] **Italian Interlude** - Alan Forest, S. African War Correspondent.

## Chapter 10

# PISA MARINA

From Viareggio's railway station it is a short walk down to the sea-side promenade, where faded chic meets colonial cutting edge. It was once the small sea port on the 10 miles of coast which belonged to the Republic of Lucca. In the 1890s it became one of the pioneer beach resorts of Europe. The renowned boat builders, who had worked mostly in wood, turned their skills to carving the ornate embellishments of the bathing establishments. The timber was harvested from the massive pine forests planted nearby. Built in Art Deco or Liberty Style, the frontages of the shops, cafes, bars and bathing establishments stood out for their individuality. They were mostly destroyed in the fire of 1917. Then came the wooden floats - huge wooden contraptions on steel chassis, which appear each year at the Carnival. Papier mache was added later.

In the 20s and 30s Viareggio became the beach capital of the Italian Riviera, with grand hotels and gardens lining the promenade. The smart set included Gabriele D'Annunzio with his lover, the flashy actress Eleanor Duse.

It is still a port of Yacht Clubs, Fish Restaurants, Marine repair yards and Boat Builders.

On the main line once again, we cruise past Puccini's Lakeside Villa, to Pisa station.

We hop onto a magic bus and follow the River Arno along the road to the sea at Pisa Marina. Nowadays it's the last outpost before you are greeted by the long line of Campervans cramming the coast roads during the summer months. They sprawl along, festooned with bicycles which dangle precariously from roof racks. The procession of nature nuts continues all the way to Livorno. This stretch of seaside is open hearted, open bloused, bronzed and brazen. Along the route, pine-wooded and art-deco campsites compete with each other for the Heidis and Helgas from Helsinki and Hamburg.

Yet Pisa Marina is still the laid-back little village where the mighty River Arno hits the sea. Five centuries ago, before the tidal silt congested the waterway, Pisa itself lay almost on the coast. Now it is 6 miles inland.

When the Arno was broad and fast flowing, it was the only outlet for both Pisa and Florence. Countless early warriors and maidens passed through here on their way to the heart of Tuscany.

As one of the 4 great Maritime City States - along with Venice, Genoa and Amalfi - Pisa became one of the most prosperous sea-republics which ruled the Mediterranean in the Middle Ages.

Earlier, Pisa and Genoa had fought side by side against the Saracen invaders. The pact between them was only scotched by an over enthusiastic Pope who promised a reward of the islands of Corsica and Sardinia to the first Republic to drive out the barbarian Moors. In order to win this valuable territory, the Pisans battled far and wide.

They even sailed down to Sicily and broke the chains of Palermo harbour, eventually driving the Saracens out of Italy altogether. At the height of her power, the Republic of Pisa ruled the coastal lands from La Spezia down to Rome, along with Sardinia, Corsica and the far off Balearic Islands.

The loser, Genoa, neither forgot nor forgave. A century later they took their revenge. They bribed the Pope and Cardinals, and laid claim to Sardinia and Corsica. Lacklustre Pisa carried on battling it out, whilst decline set in. Their fleet was destroyed at the Battle of Medusa, and the victors blocked the entrance to the Arno River with rocks. Eventually Pisa was conquered by Florence to become part of the Grand Duchy of Tuscany.

Throughout the 17th century, Florence was named 'Florentia' - derived from the name which conjures up the flower of cities all, *Florens Ensis* – 'The Sword of Flowers'. However, to ensure they were well away from their rivals, the canny Medicis turned their attention elsewhere. They made the nearby malaria infested Livorno into their own exclusive outlet to the ocean, with a free port status. All locals were barred, except their own Florentine citizens. They encouraged an influx of foreigners from far-a-field. Catholic refugees driven out of Britain & France by the Protestants, and Jews from Spain, driven out by the Catholics, arrived. Greeks, Armenians, Moors and Dutch, as well as outlaws, bandits, hookers and scum - safe from arrest in the open Free Port - were welcomed with open arms. It was the Melting Pot of the Med. By the 1600's the population was 20,000, of whom 5000 were Jewish. The rich Spanish Jews were particularly welcome as the most industrious and crafty in Europe. Livorno became the mainstay of their emigration from their homeland. *"Qui va a Liorna, ei va I no torna"* goes an old Jewish-Spanish proverb – "He who goes to Livorno will never return."

The earthy English also stamped their local accent on the map. Instead of dropping their H's, they added one. They copied the local dialect, where a 'V' is pronounced like a hard 'G.' They changed the romantic *Ligorne* to Leghorn. It sounded raunchier, and has remained ever since. Its free port status spawned a thriving merchant class, with traders importing luxuries such as English Tweed, Linens and Tea. They exported Leghorn straw hats and Leghorn cockerels. Crossbred successfully with English breeds, they were brought back from England to become the most prized poultry in Tuscany. The word 'deh' is still heard around town. It is a corruption of the English 'the'.

'Leghorn – a thriving, businesslike, matter-of-fact place, where idleness is shouldered out by commerce' commented Charles Dickens.

He was one of the first to travel there by train: "The railroad between Leghorn and Pisa is a good one and has already begun to astonish Italy with a precedent of punctuality, order, plain dealing, and improvement – the most dangerous and heretical astonisher of all".

The line was completed in 1844 by George Stephenson's son Robert as the first part of the planned link between Florence and the coast at Livorno. It was one of the earliest commercial rail lines in Italy, and was opened by the Grand Duke of Tuscany in a fanfare

172

of trumpets, gusts of steam and huge applause from the crowds on the adjacent hillside. It was also blessed by the Archbishop of Pisa who was at first sceptical, since Pope Gregory XVI had been violently opposed to new fangled inventions such as railways and street lighting. There was no further railway development in the vast, adjoining Papal States until the Pope died two years later. His trendy successor, 'Pio Nono' (Pope Pius IX) was a radical reformer. He enthusiastically encouraged all and sundry to build as many lines as possible, often through the difficult mountainous terrain of the spine of Italy.

*The joke goes that on reaching the Pearly Gates, Pope Gregory asked St. Peter if it was far to heaven, since his legs were getting tired. "Ah! said St. Peter, " If only you had built a railway; then you would have been in Paradise by now!" [1]*

"Laws in Tuscany last a week, those in Livorno last barely a day", goes an old local proverb.

Leghorn was also known as a city of violence, where murderers waylaid visiting wanderers, both on or off the beaten track.

"The most impressive thing about Leghorn is the English burial ground", added Evelyn Waugh.

Today, the Arno River at Pisa Marina has no chains across its mouth. They have been replaced by pointed fishing nets suspended on wooden frames, swung out across the waters. They are lowered into the sea to trap the autumn harvest of eels, as they migrate from fresh water to the coast. Sea bass, mullet, crabs, shrimp and flounder join the catch.

As we looked out across this almost mediaeval vista, Luigi the fisherman, with his battered three-cornered revolutionary hat, is painstaking repairing the net on one of these contraptions, which have trailed these waters for hundreds of years. He is using modern plastic thread that will stand the test of time. Alongside him, surrounded by the smart racy craft of all shapes and sizes, lie the time honoured rustic fishing smacks, with their tanned canvas sails, sharply peaked, standing rigidly to attention. He shouts and gestures rudely as a noisy motor boat moves out to sea.

We walked across to where the boat has just left the jetty. Pointing out to the tranquil ocean, the air was brooding mischievously over the mouth of this waterway. I was reminded of the countless boats that have passed by since Byron's 'Bolivar' and Shelley's 'Ariel' ploughed these same waters to their dismal destiny in the 1820s.

This little corner of Pisa Marina has kept its melancholy charm. The same buildings on the main square are still unmarred by poles or wires. It is spacious and graciousness, like a film set. You sit here at a seaside fish restaurant, enjoying the mussels and the stuffed cuttlefish and you muse.

Just across the River Arno's mouth, on the north bank, is the hunting lodge of unlucky King Victor Emmanuel, who was made Emperor of Ethiopia and King of Albania, by Mussolini. He had made an uneasy truce with Il Duce. His wife made an unsuccessful attempt to end the war between Italy and America.

He abdicated, and fled into exile in favour of his son, the equally unlucky King Umberto. Having reigned for only 33 days in 1946, he also went into exile. He stood on the runway for a last farewell at Rome's Ciampino Airport, and turned to his Secretary. "Non dimenticare I conti!" he dictated. (Don't forget the Accounts). Waving his arms towards the assembled entourage - waiting in hushed expectation - they responded in chorus: "I Conti ! The Counts! Of course, they all made themselves Counts.

The referendum was close. A majority of only 2 million voted in favour of a Republic. Some say that had his father King Victor Emmanuel abdicated earlier, it would have saved the monarchy. Others declared the referendum flawed, since millions of pro-monarchists had been unable to return home to vote. Hundreds of thousands were still interned in foreign camps. Countless others were living in territory overrun by the Yugoslavs, since Italy's fluid boundaries had not been finalised. That such a vote of important reform should be taken at such a time was a breathtaking disgrace. It presented the Monarchy as the most convenient scapegoat for everybody's crimes and mistakes. It was a vote organised by carpet baggers and anarchists who were decidedly Republican.

King Umberto was never allowed to return to the land of his birth, and died in exile in Switzerland. His legendary last three words paraphrased Byron's own: *"Italia! O Italia!"*

*'Thou who has the fatal gift of beauty'* Byron had added.

The old Royal hunting lodge is surrounded by thousands of open acres and pine forests leading down to miles of unspoilt beaches. This little coastal strip is a haven for Boars, Deer, Wildfowl, Foxes Cormorants and Herons. When a British Prime Minister came to stay here in the summer of his heyday, the Lodge was all spruced up at great expense by the local Mayor. Even though it is now a national park, open on certain days, never mind the public. It was forbidden territory. Some enterprising paparazzi took it in their stride, by the only route available – from the sea. They aimed their cameras and motor-boats straight for the shore line. When the police told them they couldn't beach, they demanded their landing rights - like all good Italian mariners, who are allowed the freedom of the first 5 metres of land from the sea.

At this spot, Gombo – midway between the mouths of the Serchio and the Arno Rivers, a body was washed up in 1822. It had been lost for 2 weeks in the ocean. The restless and reckless Percy Shelley was racing home from Leghorn with his two companions in his dodgy 30 footer, the 'Ariel', when he was caught in a storm. The Ariel was a boat of unstable design, and he had changed the name from Byron's first choice the 'Don Juan'. It was a bad omen. The weather was sultry, with no hint of an impending storm. Out of the oppressive heat of July, the Sirocco suddenly blew up.

The impulsive Percy had ignored the advice of the local fishermen and sailors, not to go out to sea. "The Devil is a-brewing mischief out there" declared one hardy mariner. With Edward Williams and a young sailor Charles Vivian, they were ten miles up the coast from Leghorn when all the other craft raced back to shore to beat the approaching Ponente, which suddenly appeared in the Gulf, having roared across from north Africa. When the storm hit them, all hell broke loose, and once again Percy was seized with suicidal tendencies. A passing Captain, seeing that their boat couldn't handle such tremendous waves, bore down on them, and offered to take them on board. He was gob smacked to hear a high-pitched voice shriek out above the raging storm: 'No!' Astonished at this stupidity, he watched through a telescope as the mountainous waves surged around them. A sailor used a speaking trumpet to shout to them to reef their sails, or they would be lost. Williams, an experienced mariner, was seen to try to lower the sails – but the impetuous Percy seized him by the arm as if in anger, and stopped him.

Captain Roberts, of the Royal Navy, was the man who had been commissioned to construct this dodgy craft at Genoa boatyards He was watching his bobbing, rolling creation through a telescope from the harbour lighthouse at Leghorn. When the storm raged past he lost site of them. Twenty minutes later nothing was seen of the Ariel. Only the other boats remained, floating around on the now calmed waters. Rumours abounded that these other boats carried Pirates, and that the 'Milord Inglese' had with him a huge booty in gold. This appealed to Italian subterfuge.

Mary Shelley had experienced that mindless spookiness of it all. Left back in Lerici with Jane Williams they were waiting for news of his return. At about half past six in the evening - the very moment that the ship had been wrecked, they had been sitting with a friend Charles Brown, on the veranda of the Casa Magni, looking directly out to sea. There was only one entrance to this terrace - a small doorway, against which one of them was seated in a chair resting firmly against the closed door. Both entry and exit were therefore impossible. Yet all three of them distinctly saw Percy in his normal clothes, with untidy hair, dashing across the terrace. They uttered a cry of joy. This turned to sadness with the sudden realisation of the impossibility of him getting either on or off the closed terrace. It slowly dawned on them that all three had seen an apparition.

On the beach at Gombo, the poet was easily identified from the English poetry book and tweed cloth of his jacket found with his body. The flesh had been eaten away, and it was unrecognisable. The bodies of his two companions were washed ashore further up the coast towards Viareggio.

Because of the quarantine regulations along the whole coast at the time, the bodies had to be buried on the beach in quicklime. Due to the timely intervention of high ranking friends, Percy's body was eventually dug up and burnt on a funeral pyre on the beach, surrounded by a group of soldiers and fashionable ladies. Byron, who had moored off shore in his yacht the Bolivar stood by. Onto the huge funeral pyre he sprinkled incense, spices and liquids in a form of poetic and pagan ritual. As the flames consumed the body a strange contest began as to who could grab the fragments of bone as likely keepsakes. Byron grabbed the skull but it fell to pieces in his hands. Hunt seized the jaw bone. What appeared to be the remains of the heart was snatched out by Trelawney who bunt his fingers. He handed it to Hunt. Mary Shelley requested this sacred relic for herself and quarrelled. It took Jane Williams to get her to surrender it. Thirty years after Mary's death the heart was discovered wrapped in silk at the bottom of her travelling desk.

At the sight of all this, Byron was sick, and swam the 3 miles from the shore back to his boat 'The Bolivar'. It was left to Trelawney to finally convey the body for burial at the English cemetery in Rome, where it lay alongside that of his son, and of John Keats, who was buried nearby.

The incorrigible old Trelawney later described it: "You can have no idea what an extraordinary effect such a funeral pyre has on a delicate shore with mountains in the background and sea before, and the singular appearance that salt and frankincense gave to the flames".

A year later, when the wreck of the boat was recovered from the sea bed, it was seen to have suffered collision damage from a felucca. In the opinion of all the expert sailors and boat builders who saw it, the craft had been run down. Williams and Shelley had attracted attention. They had fallen foul of the locals when they drew pistols on a military guard who tried to prevent them landing on a forbidden beach along the coast which was well manned by forts. Two Inglese, associated with Byron and Shelley, were also known to have attacked a guard at Pisa.

When Shelley died, the restless Byron moved on. First to Genoa, then to more revolutionary climes in Greece, which was fighting a War of independence from Turkey. He went to live on the British occupied Ionian islands whilst deciding which Greek faction to join up with. At Missolonghi he found his match; a disillusioned bunch of corrupt Greek racketeers. The place was also swarming with mosquitoes and rats carrying the plague. His loyal pet dogs probably caused his death, poisoned by tick fever. He was further weakened by the disastrous removal of almost 50 per cent of his blood by the doctors.

The swashbuckling Trelawney stayed on in Greece after Byron's death. He became an arms dealer for his Greek hero - the robber baron Odysseus. To secure his future, he had married the chief's 13 year old daughter. When Odysseus was arrested for betraying his fellow Greeks to the Turks, Trelawney was also run in, and just escaped with his life. Tired of Hellenic matters, this randy raddled rake returned to England after a colourful and dangerous career.

He married many times and had several mistresses and daughters. He proposed to Mary Shelley and had an affair with Claire Claremont. At the same time he was sleeping in Genoa with the wife of one of his friends. Still not content, he was trying to revive his liaison with a former mistress in Paris, and even asked Mary Shelley who had a good command of French, to write a letter to her to keep the old flame alive.

Fifty years on, in 1875, the Times newspaper carried a story from this incorrigible old scoundrel, who had retired to the South Coast of England. He had received a letter from his daughter, who was living in Rome. She wrote of a report that an old fisherman, who had died near Sarzana, had confessed on his death-bed that he had helped to sink Percy Shelley's boat by ramming into it. Trelawney died in 1881 and was also buried next to his hero in the English cemetery in Rome.


Our round trip had come to an end.
We had done the full circle.
English and Austrian stood on a Tuscan beach.
It said it all. The whole saga of these parts.
Inge picked up a handful of broken shells, and crunched them. Angela kicked some pebbles into the surf. It was a spirited gesture which concentrated our thoughts.
Like trespassing on the sands of time.
For revolution and civil war were no strangers to these shores.


**"Italy does not judge. It is so non moral. It is free".**
D.H.Lawrence

---

[1] As told in **Blood, Iron & Gold** by Christian Wolmar. (Atlantic Books)

# BIBLIOGRAPHY

Byron – The Years of Fame. Peter Quennell
Byron Life and Legend. Fiona MacCarthy.
Lives of the Poets. Michael Schmidt
Mary Shelley. Miranda Seymour.
Browning. Iain Finlayson.
Ghosts of the Spanish Steps. Danielle Varè
Michelangelo's Mountain. Eric Scigliano.
Napoleon Bonaparte. Robert Asprey.
Rites of Peace. Adam Zamoyski.
Florence – A Literary Companion.
Abroad – Miscellany of Travel. MacDonald.
The Italians. Luigi Barzini.
Blood, Iron and Gold. Christian Wolmar.
Italian Interlude. Alan Forest.
Buffalo Soldiers in Italy. Hondon B.Hargrove
Per Ricordare Somocolonia. Moreno Salvadori.
Marzabotto: Crimes of Walter Reder. Christian Ortner.
Italy's Sorrow. James Holland.
Days of Battle. Rick Atkinson.
Tuscany & the Gothic Line. Luciano Casella.

184